G. P. Stielinger J.

THE UNIFORM EDITION OF
THE PLAYS OF J. M. BARRIE

THE ADMIRABLE
CRICHTON

THE PLAYS OF
J. M. BARRIE

THE ADMIRABLE

CRICHTON

A COMEDY

CHARLES SCRIBNER'S SONS

NEW YORK : : : : : : : : : 1931

ACT 1

ACT I

AT LOAM HOUSE, MAYFAIR

A moment before the curtain rises, the Hon. Ernest Woolley drives up to the door of Loam House in Mayfair. There is a happy smile on his pleasant, insignificant face, and this presumably means that he is thinking of himself. He is too busy over nothing, this man about town, to be always thinking of himself, but, on the other hand, he almost never thinks of any other person. Probably Ernest's great moment is when he wakes of a morning and realises that he really is Ernest, for we must all wish to be that which is our ideal. We can conceive him springing out of bed light-heartedly and waiting for his man to do the rest. He is dressed in excellent taste, with just the little bit more which shows that he is not without a sense of humour: the dandiacal are often saved by carrying a smile at the whole thing in their spats, let us say. Ernest left Cambridge the other day, a member of the Athenæum (which he would be sorry to have you confound with a club in London of the same name). He is a bachelor, but not of arts, no mean epigrammatist (as you shall see), and a favourite of the ladies. He

3

is almost a celebrity in restaurants, where he dines frequently, returning to sup; and during this last year he has probably paid as much in them for the privilege of handing his hat to an attendant as the rent of a working-man's flat. He complains brightly that he is hard up, and that if somebody or other at Westminster does not look out the country will go to the dogs. He is no fool. He has the shrewdness to float with the current because it is a labour-saving process, but he has sufficient pluck to fight, if fight he must (a brief contest, for he would soon be toppled over). He has a light nature, which would enable him to bob up cheerily in new conditions and return unaltered to the old ones. His selfishness is his most endearing quality. If he has his way he will spend his life like a cat in pushing his betters out of the soft places, and until he is old he will be fondled in the process.

He gives his hat to one footman and his cane to another, and mounts the great staircase unassisted and undirected. As a nephew of the house he need show no credentials even to Crichton, who is guarding a door above.

It would not be good taste to describe Crichton, who is only a servant; if to the scandal of all good houses he is to stand out as a figure in the play, he must do it on his own, as they say in the pantry and the boudoir.

*We are not going to help him. We have had mis-
givings ever since we found his name in the title, and
we shall keep him out of his rights as long as we can.
Even though we softened to him he would not be a hero
in these clothes of servitude; and he loves his clothes.
How to get him out of them? It would require a
cataclysm. To be an indoor servant at all is to
Crichton a badge of honour; to be a butler at thirty
is the realisation of his proudest ambitions. He is
devotedly attached to his master, who, in his opinion,
has but one fault, he is not sufficiently contemptuous of
his inferiors. We are immediately to be introduced to
this solitary failing of a great English peer.*

*This perfect butler, then, opens a door, and ushers
Ernest into a certain room. At the same moment the
curtain rises on this room, and the play begins.*

*It is one of several reception-rooms in Loam House,
not the most magnificent but quite the softest; and of
a warm afternoon all that those who are anybody crave
for is the softest. The larger rooms are magnificent
and bare, carpetless, so that it is an accomplishment
to keep one's feet on them; they are sometimes lent for
charitable purposes; they are also all in use on the
night of a dinner-party, when you may find yourself
alone in one, having taken a wrong turning; or alone,
save for two others who are within hailing distance.*

*This room, however, is comparatively small and
very soft. There are so many cushions in it that
you wonder why, if you are an outsider and don't
know that it needs six cushions to make one fair head
comfy. The couches themselves are cushions as large
as beds, and there is an art of sinking into them and of
waiting to be helped out of them. There are several
famous paintings on the walls, of which you may say
'Jolly thing that,' without losing caste as knowing too
much; and in cases there are glorious miniatures, but
the daughters of the house cannot tell you of whom;
'there is a catalogue somewhere.' There are a
thousand or so of roses in basins, several library
novels, and a row of weekly illustrated newspapers
lying against each other like fallen soldiers. If any
one disturbs this row Crichton seems to know of it
from afar and appears noiselessly and replaces the
wanderer. One thing unexpected in such a room is
a great array of tea things. Ernest spots them with
a twinkle, and has his epigram at once unsheathed.
He dallies, however, before delivering the thrust.*

ERNEST.   I perceive, from the tea cups,
Crichton, that the great function is to take
place here.

CRICHTON (*with a respectful sigh*).   Yes, sir.

ERNEST (*chuckling heartlessly*).   The servants'
hall coming up to have tea in the drawing-room!
(*With terrible sarcasm.*)   No wonder you look
happy, Crichton.

CRICHTON (*under the knife*).   No, sir.

ERNEST.   Do you know, Crichton, I think
that with an effort you might look even happier.
(CRICHTON *smiles wanly.*)   You don't approve
of his lordship's compelling his servants to be
his equals—once a month?

CRICHTON.   It is not for me, sir, to disapprove
of his lordship's Radical views.

ERNEST.   Certainly not.   And, after all, it is
only once a month that he is affable to you.

CRICHTON.   On all other days of the month,
sir, his lordship's treatment of us is everything
that could be desired.

ERNEST.   (*This is the epigram.*)   Tea cups!
Life, Crichton, is like a cup of tea; the more
heartily we drink, the sooner we reach the
dregs.

CRICHTON (*obediently*).   Thank you, sir.

ERNEST (*becoming confidential, as we do when*

we have need of an ally). Crichton, in case I should be asked to say a few words to the servants, I have strung together a little speech. *(His hand strays to his pocket.)* I was wondering where I should stand.

> *(He tries various places and postures, and comes to rest leaning over a high chair, whence, in dumb show, he addresses a gathering.* CRICHTON, *with the best intentions, gives him a footstool to stand on, and departs, happily unconscious that* ERNEST *in some dudgeon has kicked the footstool across the room.)*

ERNEST *(addressing an imaginary audience, and desirous of startling them at once).* Suppose you were all little fishes at the bottom of the sea——

> *(He is not quite satisfied with his position, though sure that the fault must lie with the chair for being too high, not with him for being too short.* CRICHTON'S *suggestion was not perhaps a bad one after all. He lifts the stool, but hastily conceals it behind him on the entrance of the* LADIES CATHERINE

and AGATHA, *two daughters of the house.*
CATHERINE *is twenty, and* AGATHA *two
years younger. They are very fashionable
young women indeed, who might wake up
for a dance, but they are very lazy,*
CATHERINE *being two years lazier than*
AGATHA.)

ERNEST (*uneasily jocular, because he is con-
cealing the footstool*). And how are my little
friends to-day?

AGATHA (*contriving to reach a settee*). Don't
be silly, Ernest. If you want to know how we
are, we are dead. Even to think of entertaining the servants is so exhausting.

CATHERINE (*subsiding nearer the door*). Be-
sides which, we have had to decide what frocks
to take with us on the yacht, and that is such a
mental strain.

ERNEST. You poor over-worked things. (*Evidently* AGATHA *is his favourite, for he helps her to
put her feet on the settee, while* CATHERINE *has to
dispose of her own feet.*)   Rest your weary limbs.

CATHERINE (*perhaps in revenge*). But why
have you a footstool in your hand?

AGATHA.   Yes?

ERNEST.   Why? (*Brilliantly; but to be sure he has had time to think it out.*)   You see, as the servants are to be the guests I must be butler. I was practising.   This is a tray, observe.

> (*Holding the footstool as a tray, he minces across the room like an accomplished footman.   The gods favour him, for just here* LADY MARY *enters, and he holds out the footstool to her.*)

Tea, my lady?

> (LADY MARY *is a beautiful creature of twenty-two, and is of a natural hauteur which is at once the fury and the envy of her sisters.   If she chooses she can make you seem so insignificant that you feel you might be swept away with the crumb-brush. She seldom chooses, because of the trouble of preening herself as she does it; she is usually content to show that you merely tire her eyes.   She often seems to be about to go to sleep in the middle of a remark: there is quite a long and anxious pause, and then she continues, like a clock*

*that hesitates, bored in the middle of its
strike.)*

LADY MARY (*arching her brows*). It is only
you, Ernest; I thought there was some one
here (*and she also bestows herself on cushions*).

ERNEST (*a little piqued, and deserting the footstool*). Had a very tiring day also, Mary?

LADY MARY (*yawning*). Dreadfully. Been
trying on engagement-rings all the morning.

ERNEST (*who is as fond of gossip as the oldest
club member*). What's that? (*To* AGATHA.)
Is it Brocklehurst?

(*The energetic* AGATHA *nods.*)

You have given your warm young heart to
Brocky?

(LADY MARY *is impervious to his humour,
but he continues bravely.*)

I don't wish to fatigue you, Mary, by insisting
on a verbal answer, but if, without straining
yourself, you can signify Yes or No, won't
you make the effort?

(*She indolently flashes a ring on her
most important finger, and he starts
back melodramatically.*)

The ring! Then I am too late, too late! (*Fixing* LADY MARY *sternly, like a prosecuting counsel.*) May I ask, Mary, does Brocky know? Of course, it was that terrible mother of his who pulled this through. Mother does everything for Brocky. Still, in the eyes of the law you will be, not her wife, but his, and, therefore, I hold that Brocky ought to be informed. Now——

> (*He discovers that their languorous eyes have closed.*)

If you girls are shamming sleep in the expectation that I shall awaken you in the manner beloved of ladies, abandon all such hopes.

> (CATHERINE *and* AGATHA *look up without speaking.*)

LADY MARY (*speaking without looking up*). You impertinent boy.

ERNEST (*eagerly plucking another epigram from his quiver*). I knew that was it, though I don't know everything. Agatha, I 'm not young enough to know everything.

> (*He looks hopefully from one to another.*

but though they try to grasp this, his brilliance baffles them.)

AGATHA (*his secret admirer*).   *Young* enough?

ERNEST (*encouragingly*).   Don't you see? I'm not young enough to know everything.

AGATHA.   I'm sure it's awfully clever, but it's so puzzling.

(*Here* CRICHTON *ushers in an athletic, pleasant-faced young clergyman,* MR. TREHERNE, *who greets the company.*)

CATHERINE.   Ernest, say it to Mr. Treherne.

ERNEST.   Look here, Treherne, I'm not young enough to know everything.

TREHERNE.   How do you mean, Ernest?

ERNEST (*a little nettled*).   I mean what I say.

LADY MARY.   Say it again; say it more slowly.

ERNEST.   I'm—not—young—enough—to—know—everything.

TREHERNE.   *I* see.   What you really mean, my boy, is that you are not old enough to know everything.

ERNEST.   No, I don't.

TREHERNE. I assure you that 's it.

LADY MARY. Of course it is.

CATHERINE. Yes, Ernest, that 's it.

(ERNEST, *in desperation*, *appeals to* CRICHTON.)

ERNEST. I am not young enough, Crichton, to know everything.

(*It is an anxious moment, but a smile is at length extorted from* CRICHTON *as with a corkscrew.*)

CRICHTON. Thank you, sir.   (*He goes.*)

ERNEST (*relieved*). Ah, if you had that fellow's head, Treherne, you would find something better to do with it than play cricket. I hear you bowl with your head.

TREHERNE (*with proper humility*). I 'm afraid cricket is all I 'm good for, Ernest.

CATHERINE (*who thinks he has a heavenly nose*). Indeed, it isn't. You are sure to get on, Mr. Treherne.

TREHERNE. Thank you, Lady Catherine.

CATHERINE. But it was the bishop who told me so. He said a clergyman who breaks both ways is sure to get on in England.

TREHERNE. I 'm jolly glad.

(*The master of the house comes in, accompanied by* LORD BROCKLEHURST. *The* EARL OF LOAM *is a widower, a philanthropist, and a peer of advanced ideas. As a widower he is at least able to interfere in the domestic concerns of his house—to rummage in the drawers, so to speak, for which he has felt an itching all his blameless life; his philanthropy has opened quite a number of other drawers to him; and his advanced ideas have blown out his figure. He takes in all the weightiest monthly reviews, and prefers those that are uncut, because he perhaps never looks better than when cutting them; but he does not read them, and save for the cutting it would suit him as well merely to take in the covers. He writes letters to the papers, which are printed in a type to scale with himself, and he is very jealous of those other correspondents who get his type. Let laws and learning, art and commerce die, but leave the big type to an intellectual aristocracy. He is really the reformed House of Lords which will come some day.*

Young LORD BROCKLEHURST *is nothing save for his rank. You could pick him up by the handful any day in Piccadilly or Holborn, buying socks—or selling them.*)

LORD LOAM (*expansively*). You are here, Ernest. Feeling fit for the voyage, Treherne?

TREHERNE. Looking forward to it enormously.

LORD LOAM. That's right. (*He chases his children about as if they were chickens.*) Now then, Mary, up and doing, up and doing. Time we had the servants in. They enjoy it so much.

LADY MARY. They hate it.

LORD LOAM. Mary, to your duties. (*And he points severely to the tea-table.*)

ERNEST (*twinkling*). Congratulations, Brocky.

LORD BROCKLEHURST (*who detests humour*). Thanks.

ERNEST. Mother pleased?

LORD BROCKLEHURST (*with dignity*). Mother is very pleased.

ERNEST. That's good. Do you go on the yacht with us?

LORD BROCKLEHURST. Sorry I can't. And look here, Ernest, I will *not* be called Brocky.

ERNEST. Mother don't like it?

LORD BROCKLEHURST. She does not. (*He leaves* ERNEST, *who forgives him and begins to think about his speech.* CRICHTON *enters.*)

LORD LOAM (*speaking as one man to another*). We are quite ready, Crichton. (CRICHTON *is distressed.*)

LADY MARY (*sarcastically*). How Crichton enjoys it!

LORD LOAM (*frowning*). He is the only one who doesn't; pitiful creature.

CRICHTON (*shuddering under his lord's displeasure*). I can't help being a Conservative, my lord.

LORD LOAM. Be a man, Crichton. You are the same flesh and blood as myself.

CRICHTON (*in pain*). Oh, my lord!

LORD LOAM (*sharply*). Show them in;

and, by the way, they were not all here last time.

CRICHTON. All, my lord, except the merest trifles.

LORD LOAM. It must be every one. (*Lowering.*) And remember this, Crichton, for the time being you are my equal. (*Testily.*) I shall soon show you whether you are not my equal. Do as you are told.

> (CRICHTON *departs to obey, and his lordship is now a general. He has no pity for his daughters, and uses a terrible threat.*)

And girls, remember, no condescension. The first who condescends recites. (*This sends them skurrying to their labours.*)

By the way, Brocklehurst, can you do anything?

LORD BROCKLEHURST. How do you mean?

LORD LOAM. Can you do anything—with a penny or a handkerchief, make them disappear, for instance?

LORD BROCKLEHURST. Good heavens, no.

LORD LOAM. It's a pity. Every one in

our position ought to be able to do something. Ernest, I shall probably ask you to say a few words; something bright and sparkling.

ERNEST. But, my dear uncle, I have prepared nothing.

LORD LOAM. Anything impromptu will do.

ERNEST. Oh—well—if anything strikes me on the spur of the moment.

> (*He unostentatiously gets the footstool into position behind the chair.* CRICHTON *reappears to announce the guests, of whom the first is the housekeeper.*)

CRICHTON (*reluctantly*). Mrs. Perkins.

LORD LOAM (*shaking hands*). Very delighted, Mrs. Perkins. Mary, our friend, Mrs. Perkins.

LADY MARY. How do you do, Mrs. Perkins? Won't you sit here?

LORD LOAM (*threateningly*). Agatha!

AGATHA (*hastily*). How do you do? Won't you sit down?

LORD LOAM (*introducing*). Lord Brocklehurst—my valued friend, Mrs. Perkins.

> (LORD BROCKLEHURST *bows and escapes. He has to fall back on* ERNEST.)

LORD BROCKLEHURST. For heaven's sake, Ernest, don't leave me for a moment; this sort of thing is utterly opposed to all my principles.

ERNEST (*airily*). You stick to me, Brocky, and I 'll pull you through.

CRICHTON. Monsieur Fleury.

ERNEST. The chef.

LORD LOAM (*shaking hands with the chef*). Very charmed to see you, Monsieur Fleury.

FLEURY. Thank you very much.

> (FLEURY *bows to* AGATHA, *who is not effusive.*)

LORD LOAM (*warningly*). Agatha—recitation !

> (*She tosses her head, but immediately finds a seat and tea for* M. FLEURY. TREHERNE *and* ERNEST *move about, making themselves amiable.* LADY MARY *is presiding at the tea-tray.*)

CRICHTON. Mr. Rolleston.

LORD LOAM (*shaking hands with his valet*). How do you do, Rolleston?

> (CATHERINE *looks after the wants of* ROLLESTON.)

CRICHTON. Mr. Tompsett.

> (TOMPSETT, *the coachman, is received with honours, from which he shrinks.*)

CRICHTON. Miss Fisher.

> (*This superb creature is no less than* LADY MARY'S *maid, and even* LORD LOAM *is a little nervous.*)

LORD LOAM. This is a pleasure, Miss Fisher.

ERNEST (*unabashed*). If I might venture, Miss Fisher (*and he takes her unto himself*).

CRICHTON. Miss Simmons.

LORD LOAM (*to* CATHERINE'S *maid*). You are always welcome, Miss Simmons.

ERNEST (*perhaps to kindle jealousy in* MISS FISHER). At last we meet. Won't you sit down?

CRICHTON. Mademoiselle Jeanne.

LORD LOAM. Charmed to see you, Mademoiselle Jeanne.

> (*A place is found for* AGATHA'S *maid, and the scene is now an animated one; but still our host thinks his girls are not sufficiently sociable. He frowns on* LADY MARY.)

LADY MARY (*in alarm*). Mr. Treherne, this is Fisher, my maid.

LORD LOAM (*sharply*). Your what, Mary?

LADY MARY. My friend.

CRICHTON. Thomas.

LORD LOAM. How do you do, Thomas?

(*The first footman gives him a reluctant hand.*)

CRICHTON. John.

LORD LOAM. How do you do, John?

(ERNEST *signs to* LORD BROCKLEHURST, *who hastens to him.*)

ERNEST (*introducing*). Brocklehurst, this is John. I think you have already met on the door-step.

CRICHTON. Jane.

(*She comes, wrapping her hands miserably in her apron.*)

LORD LOAM (*doggedly*). Give me your hand, Jane.

CRICHTON. Gladys.

ERNEST. How do you do, Gladys. You know my uncle?

LORD LOAM. Your hand, Gladys.

(*He bestows her on* AGATHA.)

CRICHTON. Tweeny.

> (*She is a very humble and frightened kitchenmaid, of whom we are to see more.*)

LORD LOAM. So happy to see you.

FISHER. John, I saw you talking to Lord Brocklehurst just now; introduce me.

LORD BROCKLEHURST (*at the same moment to* ERNEST). That's an uncommon pretty girl; if I must feed one of them, Ernest, that's the one.

> (*But* ERNEST *tries to part him and* FISHER *as they are about to shake hands.*)

ERNEST. No you don't, it won't do, Brocky. (*To* MISS FISHER.) You are too pretty, my dear. Mother wouldn't like it. (*Discovering* TWEENY.) Here's something safer. Charming girl, Brocky, dying to know you; let me introduce you. Tweeny, Lord Brocklehurst— Lord Brocklehurst, Tweeny.

> (BROCKLEHURST *accepts his fate; but he still has an eye for* FISHER, *and something may come of this.*)

LORD LOAM (*severely*). They are not all here, Crichton.

CRICHTON (*with a sigh*).   Odds and ends.

(*A* STABLE-BOY *and a* PAGE *are shown in, and for a moment no daughter of the house advances to them.*)

LORD LOAM (*with a roving eye on his children*).   Which is to recite?

(*The last of the company are, so to say, embraced.*)

LORD LOAM (*to* TOMPSETT, *as they partake of tea together*).   And how are all at home?

TOMPSETT.   Fairish, my lord, if 'tis the horses you are inquiring for?

LORD LOAM.   No, no, the family. How's the baby?

TOMPSETT.   Blooming, your lordship.

LORD LOAM.   A very fine boy. I remember saying so when I saw him; nice little fellow.

TOMPSETT (*not quite knowing whether to let it pass*).   Beg pardon, my lord, it's a girl.

LORD LOAM.   A girl? Aha! ha! ha! exactly what I said. I distinctly remember saying, If it's spared it will be a girl.

(CRICHTON *now comes down.*)

LORD LOAM. Very delighted to see you, Crichton.

(CRICHTON *has to shake hands.*)

Mary, you know Mr. Crichton?

(*He wanders off in search of other prey.*)

LADY MARY. Milk and sugar, Crichton?

CRICHTON. I'm ashamed to be seen talking to you, my lady.

LADY MARY. To such a perfect servant as you all this must be most distasteful. (CRICHTON *is too respectful to answer.*) Oh, please to speak, or I shall have to recite. You do hate it, don't you?

CRICHTON. It pains me, your ladyship. It disturbs the etiquette of the servants' hall. After last month's meeting the pageboy, in a burst of equality, called me Crichton. He was dismissed.

LADY MARY. I wonder—I really do—how you can remain with us.

CRICHTON. I should have felt compelled to give notice, my lady, if the master had not had a seat in the Upper House. I cling to that.

LADY MARY. Do go on speaking. Tell me,

what did Mr. Ernest mean by saying he was not young enough to know everything?

CRICHTON.   I have no idea, my lady.

LADY MARY.   But you laughed.

CRICHTON.   My lady, he is the second son of a peer.

LADY MARY.   Very proper sentiments. You are a good soul, Crichton.

LORD BROCKLEHURST (*desperately to* TWEENY). And now tell me, have you been to the Opera? What sort of weather have you been having in the kitchen?   (TWEENY *gurgles.*)   For Heaven's sake, woman, be articulate.

CRICHTON (*still talking to* LADY MARY).   No, my lady; his lordship may compel us to be equal   upstairs, but there will never be equality in the servants' hall.

LORD LOAM (*overhearing this*).   What's that? No equality?   Can't you see, Crichton, that our divisions into classes are artificial, that if we were to return to Nature, which is the aspiration of my life, all would be equal?

CRICHTON.   If I may make so bold as to contradict your lordship——

LORD LOAM (*with an effort*).   Go on.

CRICHTON.   The divisions into classes, my lord, are not artificial.   They are the natural outcome of a civilised society.   (*To* LADY MARY.)   There must always be a master and servants in all civilised communities, my lady, for it is natural, and whatever is natural is right.

LORD LOAM (*wincing*).   It is very unnatural for me to stand here and allow you to talk such nonsense.

CRICHTON (*eagerly*).   Yes, my lord, it is. That is what I have been striving to point out to your lordship.

AGATHA (*to* CATHERINE).   What is the matter with Fisher?   She is looking daggers.

CATHERINE.   The tedious creature; some question of etiquette, I suppose.

(*She sails across to* FISHER.)

How are you, Fisher?

FISHER (*with a toss of her head*).   I am nothing, my lady, I am nothing at all.

AGATHA.   Oh dear, who says so?

FISHER (*affronted*).   His lordship has asked

that kitchen wench to have a second cup of tea.

CATHERINE. But why not?

FISHER. If it pleases his lordship to offer it to *her* before offering it to *me*——

AGATHA. So that is it. Do you want another cup of tea, Fisher?

FISHER. No, my lady—but my position—I should have been asked first.

AGATHA. Oh dear.

> (*All this has taken some time, and by now the feeble appetites of the uncomfortable guests have been satiated. But they know there is still another ordeal to face—his lordship's monthly speech. Every one awaits it with misgiving—the servants lest they should applaud, as last time, in the wrong place, and the daughters because he may be personal about them, as the time before.* ERNEST *is annoyed that there should be this speech at all when there is such a much better one coming, and* BROCKLEHURST *foresees the degradation of the peerage. All are thinking*

of themselves alone save CRICHTON, *who
knows his master's weakness, and fears
he may stick in the middle.* LORD LOAM,
*however, advances cheerfully to his doom.
He sees* ERNEST'S *stool, and artfully
stands on it, to his nephew's natural
indignation. The three ladies knit their
lips, the servants look down their noses,
and the address begins.*)

LORD LOAM. My friends, I am glad to see
you all looking so happy. It used to be pre-
dicted by the scoffer that these meetings would
prove distasteful to you. Are they distasteful?
I hear you laughing at the question.

(*He has not heard them, but he hears
them now, the watchful* CRICHTON *giving
them a lead.*)

No harm in saying that among us to-day is
one who was formerly hostile to the move-
ment, but who to-day has been won over.
I refer to Lord Brocklehurst, who, I am
sure, will presently say to me that if the
charming lady now by his side has derived
as much pleasure from his company as he

has derived from hers, he will be more than satisfied.

(*All look at* TWEENY, *who trembles.*)

For the time being the artificial and unnatural —I say unnatural (*glaring at* CRICHTON, *who bows slightly*)—barriers of society are swept away. Would that they could be swept away for ever.

> (*The* PAGEBOY *cheers, and has the one moment of prominence in his life. He grows up, marries and has children, but is never really heard of again.*)

But that is entirely and utterly out of the question. And now for a few months we are to be separated. As you know, my daughters and Mr. Ernest and Mr. Treherne are to accompany me on my yacht, on a voyage to distant parts of the earth. In less than forty-eight hours we shall be under weigh.

> (*But for* CRICHTON's *eye the reckless* PAGEBOY *would repeat his success.*)

Do not think our life on the yacht is to be one long idle holiday. My views on the excessive luxury of the day are well known, and what

I preach I am resolved to practise. I have
therefore decided that my daughters, instead
of having one maid each as at present, shall on
this voyage have but one maid between them.

(*Three maids rise; also three mistresses.*)

CRICHTON. My lord!

LORD LOAM. My mind is made up.

ERNEST. I cordially agree.

LORD LOAM. And now, my friends, I should
like to think that there is some piece of advice
I might give you, some thought, some noble
saying over which you might ponder in my
absence. In this connection I remember a
proverb, which has had a great effect on my
own life. I first heard it many years ago. I
have never forgotten it. It constantly cheers
and guides me. That proverb is—that proverb
was—the proverb I speak of——

(*He grows pale and taps his forehead.*)

LADY MARY. Oh dear, I believe he has forgotten it.

LORD LOAM (*desperately*). The proverb—
that proverb to which I refer——

(*Alas, it has gone. The distress is*

*general. He has not even the sense to sit
down. He gropes for the proverb in the
air. They try applause, but it is no help.)*
I have it now—(*not he*).

LADY MARY (*with confidence*).   Crichton.

*(He does not fail her. As quietly as if
he were in goloshes, mind as well as
feet, he dismisses the domestics; they
go according to precedence as they entered,
yet, in a moment, they are gone. Then
he signs to* MR. TREHERNE, *and they
conduct* LORD LOAM *with dignity from
the room. His hands are still catching
flies; he still mutters, 'The proverb—
that proverb'; but he continues, owing
to* CRICHTON'S *skilful treatment, to look
every inch a peer. The ladies have now
an opportunity to air their indignation.)*

LADY MARY.   One maid among three grown
women!

LORD BROCKLEHURST.   Mary, I think I had
better go.   That dreadful kitchenmaid——

LADY MARY.   I can't blame you, George.

(He salutes her.)

LORD BROCKLEHURST. Your father's views are shocking to me, and I am glad I am not to be one of the party on the yacht. My respect for myself, Mary, my natural anxiety as to what mother will say. I shall see you, darling, before you sail.

(*He bows to the others and goes.*)

ERNEST. Selfish brute, only thinking of himself. What about my speech?

LADY MARY. One maid among three of us. What's to be done?

ERNEST. Pooh! You must do for yourselves, that's all.

LADY MARY. Do for ourselves. How can we know where our things are kept?

AGATHA. Are you aware that dresses button up the back?

CATHERINE. How are we to get into our shoes and be prepared for the carriage?

LADY MARY. Who is to put us to bed, and who is to get us up, and how shall we ever know it's morning if there is no one to pull up the blinds?

(CRICHTON *crosses on his way out.*)

ERNEST.   How is his lordship now?

CRICHTON.   A little easier, sir.

LADY MARY.   Crichton, send Fisher to me.
(*He goes.*)

ERNEST.   I have no pity for you girls, I——

LADY MARY.   Ernest, go away, and don't
insult the broken-hearted.

ERNEST.   And uncommon glad I am to go.
Ta-ta, all o' you.   He asked me to say a few
words.   I came here to say a few words, and
I'm not at all sure that I couldn't bring an
action against him.

> (*He departs, feeling that he has left a
> dart behind him.   The girls are alone
> with their tragic thoughts.*)

LADY MARY (*become a mother to the younger
ones at last*).   My poor sisters, come here.   (*They
go to her doubtfully.*)   We must make this draw
us closer together.   I shall do my best to help
you in every way.   Just now I cannot think
of myself at all.

AGATHA.   But how unlike you, Mary.

LADY MARY.   It is my duty to protect my
sisters.

CATHERINE. I never knew her so sweet before, Agatha. (*Cautiously.*) What do you propose to do, Mary?

LADY MARY. I propose when we are on the yacht to lend Fisher to you when I don't need her myself.

AGATHA. Fisher?

LADY MARY (*who has the most character of the three*). Of course, as the eldest, I have decided that it is *my* maid we shall take with us.

CATHERINE (*speaking also for* AGATHA). Mary, you toad.

AGATHA. Nothing on earth would induce Fisher to lift her hand for either me or Catherine.

LADY MARY. I was afraid of it, Agatha. That is why I am so sorry for you.

(*The further exchange of pleasantries is interrupted by the arrival of* FISHER.)

LADY MARY. Fisher, you heard what his lordship said?

FISHER. Yes, my lady.

LADY MARY (*coldly, though the others would have tried blandishment*). You have given me some satisfaction of late, Fisher, and to mark my approval I have decided that you shall be the maid who accompanies us.

FISHER (*acidly*).   I thank you, my lady.

LADY MARY.   That is all; you may go.

FISHER (*rapping it out*).   If you please, my lady, I wish to give notice.

> (CATHERINE *and* AGATHA *gleam, but* LADY MARY *is of sterner stuff.*)

LADY MARY (*taking up a book*).   Oh, certainly —you may go.

CATHERINE.   But why, Fisher?

FISHER.   I could not undertake, my lady, to wait upon three. *We* don't do it. (*In an indignant outburst to* LADY MARY.)   Oh, my lady, to think that this affront——

LADY MARY (*looking up*).   I thought I told you to go, Fisher.

> (FISHER *stands for a moment irresolute; then goes. As soon as she has gone* LADY MARY *puts down her book and weeps. She is a pretty woman, but this is the only pretty thing we have seen her do yet.*)

AGATHA (*succinctly*).   Serves you right.

(CRICHTON *comes.*)

CATHERINE.   It will be Simmons after all.
Send Simmons to me.

CRICHTON (*after hesitating*).   My lady, might
I venture to speak?

CATHERINE.   What is it?

CRICHTON.   I happen to know, your ladyship,
that Simmons desires to give notice for the same
reason as Fisher.

CATHERINE.   Oh!

AGATHA (*triumphant*).   Then, Catherine, we
take Jeanne.

CRICHTON.   And Jeanne also, my lady.

(LADY MARY *is reading, indifferent though
the heavens fall, but her sisters are not
ashamed to show their despair to* CRICHTON.)

AGATHA.   We can't blame them.   Could any
maid who respected herself be got to wait upon
three?

LADY MARY (*with languid interest*).   I suppose
there are such persons, Crichton?

CRICHTON (*guardedly*).   I have heard, my
lady, that there are such.

LADY MARY (*a little desperate*). Crichton, what's to be done? We sail in two days; could one be discovered in the time?

AGATHA (*frankly a supplicant*). Surely you can think of some one?

CRICHTON (*after hesitating*). There is in this establishment, your ladyship, a young woman——

LADY MARY. Yes?

CRICHTON. A young woman, on whom I have for some time cast an eye.

CATHERINE (*eagerly*). Do you mean as a possible lady's-maid?

CRICHTON. I had thought of her, my lady, in another connection.

LADY MARY. Ah!

CRICHTON. But I believe she is quite the young person you require. Perhaps if you could see her, my lady——

LADY MARY. I shall certainly see her. Bring her to me. (*He goes.*) You two needn't wait.

CATHERINE. Needn't we? We see your little game, Mary.

AGATHA. We shall certainly remain and have our two-thirds of her.

(*They sit there doggedly until* CRICHTON *returns with* TWEENY, *who looks scared.*)

CRICHTON. This, my lady, is the young person.

CATHERINE (*frankly*). Oh dear!

(*It is evident that all three consider her quite unsuitable.*)

LADY MARY. Come here, girl. Don't be afraid.

(TWEENY *looks imploringly at her idol.*)

CRICHTON. Her appearance, my lady, is homely, and her manners, as you may have observed, deplorable, but she has a heart of gold.

LADY MARY. What is your position down-stairs?

TWEENY (*bobbing*). I'm a tweeny, your ladyship.

CATHERINE. A what?

CRICHTON. A tweeny; that is to say, my lady, she is not at present, strictly speaking, anything; a *between* maid; she helps the vegetable maid. It is she, my lady, who conveys the dishes from the one end of the kitchen table, where they are placed by the cook, to the other end, where they enter into the charge of Thomas and John.

LADY MARY. I see. And you and Crichton are—ah—keeping company?

(CRICHTON *draws himself up.*)

TWEENY (*aghast*). A butler don't keep company, my lady.

LADY MARY (*indifferently*). Does he not?

CRICHTON. No, your ladyship, we butlers may—(*he makes a gesture with his arms*)—but we do not keep company.

AGATHA. I know what it is; you are engaged?

(TWEENY *looks longingly at* CRICHTON.)

CRICHTON. Certainly not, my lady. The utmost I can say at present is that I have cast a favourable eye.

(*Even this is much to* TWEENY.)

LADY MARY. As you choose. But I am afraid, Crichton, she will not suit us.

CRICHTON. My lady, beneath this simple

exterior are concealed a very sweet nature and rare womanly gifts.

AGATHA.   Unfortunately, that is not what we want.

CRICHTON.   And it is she, my lady, who dresses the hair of the ladies'-maids for our evening meals.

(*The ladies are interested at last.*)

LADY MARY.   She dresses Fisher's hair?

TWEENY.   Yes, my lady, and I does them up when they goes to parties.

CRICHTON (*pained, but not scolding*).   *Does!*

TWEENY.   Doos.   And it's me what alters your gowns to fit them.

CRICHTON.   *What* alters!

TWEENY.   Which alters.

AGATHA.   Mary?

LADY MARY.   I shall certainly have her.

CATHERINE.   *We* shall certainly have her. Tweeny, we have decided to make a lady's-maid of you.

TWEENY.   Oh lawks!

AGATHA.   We are doing this for you so that your position socially may be more nearly akin to that of Crichton.

CRICHTON (*gravely*). It will undoubtedly increase the young person's chances.

LADY MARY. Then if I get a good character for you from Mrs. Perkins, she will make the necessary arrangements.

(*She resumes reading.*)

TWEENY (*elated*). My lady!

LADY MARY. By the way, I hope you are a good sailor.

TWEENY (*startled*). You don't mean, my lady, I 'm to go on the ship?

LADY MARY. Certainly.

TWEENY. But— (*To* CRICHTON.) You ain't going, sir?

CRICHTON. No.

TWEENY (*firm at last*). Then neither ain't I.

AGATHA. You must.

TWEENY. Leave him! Not me.

LADY MARY. Girl, don't be silly. Crichton will be—considered in your wages.

TWEENY. I ain't going.

CRICHTON. I feared this, my lady.

TWEENY. Nothing 'll budge me.

LADY MARY.   Leave the room.

(CRICHTON *shows* TWEENY *out with marked politeness.*)

AGATHA.   Crichton, I think you might have shown more displeasure with her.

CRICHTON (*contrite*).   I was touched, my lady. I see, my lady, that to part from her would be a wrench to me, though I could not well say so in her presence, not having yet decided how far I shall go with her.

(*He is about to go when* LORD LOAM *returns, fuming.*)

LORD LOAM. The ingrate! The smug! The fop!

CATHERINE.   What is it now, father?

LORD LOAM.   That man of mine, Rolleston, refuses to accompany us because you are to have but one maid.

AGATHA.   Hurrah!

LADY MARY (*in better taste*).   Darling father, rather than you should lose Rolleston, we will consent to take all the three of them.

LORD LOAM.   Pooh, nonsense! Crichton, find me a valet who can do without three maids.

CRICHTON.   Yes, my lord. (*Troubled.*) In the

time—the more suitable the party, my lord, the less willing will he be to come without the—the usual perquisites.

LORD LOAM. Any one will do.

CRICHTON (*shocked*). My lord!

LORD LOAM. The ingrate! The puppy!

> (AGATHA *has an idea, and whispers to* LADY MARY.)

LADY MARY. I ask a favour of a servant?—never!

AGATHA. Then I will. Crichton, would it not be very distressing to you to let his lordship go, attended by a valet who might prove unworthy? It is only for three months; don't you think that you—you yourself—you——

> (*As* CRICHTON *sees what she wants he pulls himself up with noble, offended dignity, and she is appalled.*)

I beg your pardon.

> (*He bows stiffly.*)

CATHERINE (*to* CRICHTON). But think of the joy to Tweeny.

> (CRICHTON *is moved, but he shakes his head.*)

LADY MARY (*so much the cleverest*). Crichton, do you think it safe to let the master you love go so far away without you while he has these dangerous views about equality?

> (CRICHTON *is profoundly stirred. After a struggle he goes to his master, who has been pacing the room.*)

CRICHTON. My lord, I have found a man.

LORD LOAM. Already? Who is he?

> (CRICHTON *presents himself with a gesture.*)

Yourself?

CATHERINE. Father, how good of him.

LORD LOAM (*pleased, but thinking it a small thing*). Uncommon good. Thank you, Crichton. This helps me nicely out of a hole; and how it will annoy Rolleston! Come with me, and we shall tell him. Not that I think you have lowered yourself in any way. Come along.

> (*He goes, and* CRICHTON *is to follow him, but is stopped by* AGATHA *impulsively offering him her hand.*)

CRICHTON (*who is much shaken*). My lady—
a valet's hand!

AGATHA. I had no idea you would feel it so
deeply; why did you do it?

(CRICHTON *is too respectful to reply.*)

LADY MARY (*regarding him*). Crichton, I am
curious. I insist upon an answer.

CRICHTON. My lady, I am the son of a butler
and a lady's-maid—perhaps the happiest of all
combinations, and to me the most beautiful
thing in the world is a haughty, aristocratic
English house, with every one kept in his
place. Though I were equal to your ladyship, where would be the pleasure to me?
It would be counterbalanced by the pain
of feeling that Thomas and John were equal
to me.

CATHERINE. But father says if we were to
return to Nature——

CRICHTON. If we did, my lady, the first
thing we should do would be to elect a head.
Circumstances might alter cases; the same
person might not be master; the same persons
might not be servants. I can't say as to that,

nor should we have the deciding of it.   Nature would decide for us.

LADY MARY.   You seem to have thought it all out carefully, Crichton.

CRICHTON.   Yes, my lady.

CATHERINE.   And you have done this for us, Crichton, because you thought that—that father needed to be kept in his place?

CRICHTON.   I should prefer you to say, my lady, that I have done it for the house.

AGATHA.   Thank you, Crichton.   Mary, be nicer to him.   (*But* LADY MARY *has begun to read again.*)   If there was any way in which we could show our gratitude.

CRICHTON.   If I might venture, my lady, would you kindly show it by becoming more like Lady Mary.   That disdain is what we like from our superiors.   Even so do we, the upper servants, disdain the lower servants, while they take it out of the odds and ends.

(*He goes, and they bury themselves in cushions.*)

AGATHA.   Oh dear, what a tiring day.

CATHERINE.   I feel dead.   Tuck in your feet,
you selfish thing.

> (LADY MARY *is lying reading on another
> couch.*)

LADY MARY.   I wonder what he meant by
circumstances might alter cases.

AGATHA (*yawning*).   Don't talk, Mary, I was
nearly asleep.

LADY MARY.   I wonder what he meant by
the same person might not be master, and the
same persons might not be servants.

CATHERINE.   Do be quiet, Mary, and leave it
to Nature;   he said Nature would decide.

LADY MARY.   I wonder——

> (*But she does not wonder very much.
> She would wonder more if she knew
> what was coming. Her book slips un-
> regarded to the floor. The ladies are at
> rest until it is time to dress.*)

End of Act I.

ACT II

ACT II

THE ISLAND

Two months have elapsed, and the scene is a desert island in the Pacific, on which our adventurers have been wrecked.

The curtain rises on a sea of bamboo, which shuts out all view save the foliage of palm trees and some gaunt rocks. Occasionally Crichton and Treherne come momentarily into sight, hacking and hewing the bamboo, through which they are making a clearing between the ladies and the shore; and by and by, owing to their efforts, we shall have an unrestricted outlook on to a sullen sea that is at present hidden. Then we shall also be able to note a mast standing out of the water—all that is left, saving floating wreckage, of the ill-fated yacht the Bluebell. *The beginnings of a hut will also be seen, with Crichton driving its walls into the ground or astride its roof of saplings, for at present he is doing more than one thing at a time. In a red shirt, with the ends of his sailor's breeches thrust into wading-boots, he looks a man for the moment; we*

51

suddenly remember some one's saying—perhaps it was ourselves—that a cataclysm would be needed to get him out of his servant's clothes, and apparently it has been forthcoming. It is no longer beneath our dignity to cast an inquiring eye on his appearance. His features are not distinguished, but he has a strong jaw and green eyes, in which a yellow light burns that we have not seen before. His dark hair, hitherto so decorously sleek, has been ruffled this way and that by wind and weather, as if they were part of the cataclysm and wanted to help his chance. His muscles must be soft and flabby still, but though they shriek aloud to him to desist, he rains lusty blows with his axe, like one who has come upon the open for the first time in his life, and likes it. He is as yet far from being an expert woodsman—mark the blood on his hands at places where he has hit them instead of the tree; but note also that he does not waste time in bandaging them—he rubs them in the earth and goes on. His face is still of the discreet pallor that befits a butler, and he carries the smaller logs as if they were a salver; not in a day or a month will he shake off the badge of servitude, but without knowing it he has begun.

But for the hatchets at work, and an occasional something horrible falling from a tree into the ladies'

*laps, they hear nothing save the mournful surf breaking
on a coral shore.*

*They sit or recline huddled together against a rock,
and they are farther from home, in every sense of the
word, than ever before. Thirty-six hours ago, they
were given three minutes in which to dress, without a
maid, and reach the boats, and they have not made the
best of that valuable time. None of them has boots,
and had they known this prickly island they would
have thought first of boots. They have a sufficiency
of garments, but some of them were gifts dropped
into the boat—Lady Mary's tarpaulin coat and hat,
for instance, and Catherine's blue jersey and red cap,
which certify that the two ladies were lately before
the mast. Agatha is too gay in Ernest's dressing-
gown, and clutches it to her person with both hands
as if afraid that it may be claimed by its rightful
owner. There are two pairs of bath slippers between
the three of them, and their hair cries aloud and in
vain for hairpins.*

*By their side, on an inverted bucket, sits Ernest,
clothed neatly in the garments of day and night, but,
alas, bare-footed. He is the only cheerful member of
this company of four, but his brightness is due less to
a manly desire to succour the helpless than to his
having been lately in the throes of composition, and to*

*his modest satisfaction with the result.   He reads to
the ladies, and they listen, each with one scared eye to
the things that fall from trees.*

ERNEST (*who has written on the fly-leaf of the
only book saved from the wreck*).   This is what
I have written.   'Wrecked, wrecked, wrecked!
on an island in the Tropics, the following:
the Hon. Ernest Woolley, the Rev. John
Treherne, the Ladies Mary, Catherine, and
Agatha Lasenby, with two servants.   We are
the sole survivors of Lord Loam's steam yacht
Bluebell, which encountered a fearful gale in
these seas, and soon became a total wreck.
The crew behaved gallantly, putting us all
into the first boat.   What became of them I
cannot tell, but we, after dreadful sufferings,
and insufficiently clad, in whatever garments
we could lay hold of in the dark'——

LADY MARY.   Please don't describe our garments.

ERNEST.   —'succeeded in reaching this island,
with the loss of only one of our party,
namely, Lord Loam, who flung away his life in

a gallant attempt to save a servant who had
fallen overboard.'

> (*The ladies have wept long and sore for
> their father, but there is something in
> this last utterance that makes them look
> up.*)

AGATHA.   But, Ernest, it was Crichton who
jumped overboard trying to save father.

ERNEST (*with the candour that is one of his
most engaging qualities*).   Well, you know, it
was rather silly of uncle to fling away his life
by trying to get into the boat first; and as
this document may be printed in the English
papers, it struck me, an English peer, you
know——

LADY MARY (*every inch an English peer's
daughter*).   Ernest, that is very thoughtful
of you.

ERNEST (*continuing, well pleased*).   —'By
night the cries of wild cats and the hissing of
snakes terrify us extremely'—(*this does not
satisfy him so well, and he makes a correction*)—
'terrify the ladies extremely.   Against these
we have no weapons except one cutlass and a

hatchet. A bucket washed ashore is at present our only comfortable seat'——

LADY MARY (*with some spirit*). And Ernest is sitting on it.

ERNEST. H'sh! Oh, do be quiet. —'To add to our horrors, night falls suddenly in these parts, and it is then that savage animals begin to prowl and roar.'

LADY MARY. Have you said that vampire bats suck the blood from our toes as we sleep?

ERNEST. No, that's all. I end up, 'Rescue us or we perish. Rich reward. Signed Ernest Woolley, in command of our little party.' This is written on a leaf taken out of a book of poems that Crichton found in his pocket. Fancy Crichton being a reader of poetry. Now I shall put it into the bottle and fling it into the sea.

> (*He pushes the precious document into a soda-water bottle, and rams the cork home. At the same moment, and without effort, he gives birth to one of his most characteristic epigrams.*)

The tide is going out, we mustn't miss the post.

(*They are so unhappy that they fail to grasp it, and a little petulantly he calls for* CRICHTON, *ever his stand-by in the hour of epigram.* CRICHTON *breaks through the undergrowth quickly, thinking the ladies are in danger.*)

CRICHTON. Anything wrong, sir?

ERNEST (*with fine confidence*). The tide, Crichton, is a postman who calls at our island twice a day for letters.

CRICHTON (*after a pause*). Thank you, sir.

(*He returns to his labours, however, without giving the smile which is the epigram-matist's right, and* ERNEST *is a little disappointed in him.*)

ERNEST. Poor Crichton! I sometimes think he is losing his sense of humour. Come along, Agatha.

(*He helps his favourite up the rocks, and they disappear gingerly from view.*)

CATHERINE. How horribly still it is.

LADY MARY (*remembering some recent sounds*). It is best when it is still.

CATHERINE (*drawing closer to her*). Mary, I

have heard that they are always very still just before they jump.

LADY MARY. Don't. (*A distinct chopping is heard, and they are startled.*)

LADY MARY (*controlling herself*). It is only Crichton knocking down trees.

CATHERINE (*almost imploringly*). Mary, let us go and stand beside him.

LADY MARY (*coldly*). Let a servant see that I am afraid!

CATHERINE. Don't, then; but remember this, dear, they often drop on one from above.

> (*She moves away, nearer to the friendly sound of the axe, and* LADY MARY *is left alone. She is the most courageous of them as well as the haughtiest, but when something she had thought to be a stick glides toward her, she forgets her dignity and screams.*)

LADY MARY (*calling*). Crichton, Crichton!

> (*It must have been* TREHERNE *who was tree-felling, for* CRICHTON *comes to her from the hut, drawing his cutlass.*)

CRICHTON (*anxious*).　Did you call, my lady?

LADY MARY (*herself again, now that he is there*).　I!　Why should I?

CRICHTON.　I made a mistake, your ladyship. (*Hesitating.*)　If you are afraid of being alone, my lady——

LADY MARY.　Afraid!　Certainly not.　(*Doggedly.*)　You may go.

> (*But she does not complain when he remains within eyesight cutting the bamboo. It is heavy work, and she watches him silently.*)

LADY MARY.　I wish, Crichton, you could work without getting so hot.

CRICHTON (*mopping his face*).　I wish I could, my lady.

> (*He continues his labours.*)

LADY MARY (*taking off her oilskins*).　It makes me hot to look at you.

CRICHTON.　It almost makes me cool to look at your ladyship.

LADY MARY (*who perhaps thinks he is presuming*).　Anything I can do for you in that way, Crichton, I shall do with pleasure.

CRICHTON (*quite humbly*). Thank you, my lady.
(*By this time most of the bamboo has
been cut, and the shore and sea are visible,
except where they are hidden by the half
completed hut. The mast rising solitary
from the water adds to the desolation of
the scene, and at last tears run down* LADY
MARY'S *face*.)

CRICHTON.   Don't give way, my lady, things
might be worse.

LADY MARY.   My poor father.

CRICHTON.   If I could have given my life for
his.

LADY MARY.   You did all a man could do.
Indeed I thank you, Crichton. (*With some
admiration and more wonder*.)   You are a man.

CRICHTON.   Thank you, my lady.

LADY MARY.   But it is all so awful.   Crichton,
is there any hope of a ship coming?

CRICHTON (*after hesitation*).   Of course there
is, my lady.

LADY MARY (*facing him bravely*).   Don't
treat me as a child.   I have got to know the
worst, and to face it.   Crichton, the truth.

CRICHTON (*reluctantly*).   We were driven out of our course, my lady; I fear far from the track of commerce.

LADY MARY.   Thank you; I understand.

> (*For a moment, however, she breaks down. Then she clenches her hands and stands erect.*)

CRICHTON (*watching her, and forgetting perhaps for the moment that they are not just a man and woman*).   You 're a good pluckt 'un, my lady.

LADY MARY (*falling into the same error*).   I shall try to be.   (*Extricating herself.*)   Crichton, how dare you?

CRICHTON.   I beg your ladyship's pardon: but you are.

> (*She smiles, as if it were a comfort to be told this even by* CRICHTON.)

And until a ship comes we are three men who are going to do our best for you ladies.

LADY MARY (*with a curl of the lip*).   Mr. Ernest does no work.

CRICHTON (*cheerily*).   But he will, my lady.

LADY MARY.   I doubt it.

CRICHTON (*confidently, but perhaps thoughtlessly*). No work—no dinner—will make a great change in Mr. Ernest.

LADY MARY. No work—no dinner. When did you invent that rule, Crichton?

CRICHTON (*loaded with bamboo*). I didn't invent it, my lady. I seem to see it growing all over the island.

LADY MARY (*disquieted*). Crichton, your manner strikes me as curious.

CRICHTON (*pained*). I hope not, your ladyship.

LADY MARY (*determined to have it out with him*). You are not implying anything so unnatural, I presume, as that if I and my sisters don't work there will be no dinner for *us*?

CRICHTON (*brightly*). If it is unnatural, my lady, that is the end of it.

LADY MARY. If? Now I understand. The perfect servant at home holds that we are all equal now. I see.

CRICHTON (*wounded to the quick*). My lady, can you think me so inconsistent?

LADY MARY. That is it.

CRICHTON (*earnestly*). My lady, I disbelieved in equality at home because it was against nature, and for that same reason I as utterly disbelieve in it on an island.

LADY MARY (*relieved by his obvious sincerity*). I apologise.

CRICHTON (*continuing unfortunately*). There must always, my lady, be one to command and others to obey.

LADY MARY (*satisfied*). One to command, others to obey. Yes. (*Then suddenly she realises that there may be a dire meaning in his confident words.*) Crichton!

CRICHTON (*who has intended no dire meaning*). What is it, my lady?

(*But she only stares into his face and then hurries from him. Left alone he is puzzled, but being a practical man he busies himself gathering firewood, until* TWEENY *appears excitedly carrying cocoa-nuts in her skirt. She has made better use than the ladies of her three minutes' grace for dressing.*)

TWEENY (*who can be happy even on an island if* CRICHTON *is with her*). Look what I found.

CRICHTON. Cocoa-nuts. Bravo!

TWEENY. They grows on trees.

CRICHTON. Where did you think they grew?

TWEENY. I thought as how they grew in rows on top of little sticks.

CRICHTON (*wrinkling his brows*). Oh Tweeny, Tweeny!

TWEENY (*anxiously*). Have I offended of your feelings again, sir?

CRICHTON. A little.

TWEENY (*in a despairing outburst*). I 'm full o' vulgar words and ways; and though I may keep them in their holes when you are by, as soon as I 'm by myself out they comes in a rush like beetles when the house is dark. I says them gloating-like, in my head—'Blooming' I says, and 'All my eye,' and 'Ginger,' and 'Nothink'; and all the time we was being wrecked I was praying to myself, 'Please the Lord it may be an island as it 's natural to be vulgar on.'

(*A shudder passes through* CRICHTON, *and she is abject.*)

That's the kind I am, sir. I'm 'opeless.
You'd better give me up.

> (*She is a pathetic, forlorn creature, and
> his manhood is stirred.*)

CRICHTON (*wondering a little at himself for
saying it*). I won't give you up. It is strange
that one so common should attract one so
fastidious; but so it is. (*Thoughtfully.*) There
is something about you, Tweeny, there is a *je ne
sais quoi* about you.

TWEENY (*knowing only that he has found
something in her to commend*). Is there, is there?
Oh, I am glad.

CRICHTON (*putting his hand on her shoulder like
a protector*). We shall fight your vulgarity
together. (*All this time he has been arranging
sticks for his fire.*) Now get some dry grass.

> (*She brings him grass, and he puts it under
> the sticks. He produces an odd lens from
> his pocket, and tries to focus the sun's
> rays.*)

TWEENY. Why, what's that?

CRICHTON (*the ingenious creature*). That's
the glass from my watch and one from Mr.

Treherne's, with a little water between them.
I'm hoping to kindle a fire with it.

TWEENY (*properly impressed*).   Oh sir!

> (*After one failure the grass takes fire,
> and they are blowing on it when excited
> cries near by bring them sharply to their
> feet.   AGATHA runs to them, white of face,
> followed by ERNEST.*)

ERNEST.   Danger!   Crichton, a tiger-cat!

CRICHTON (*getting his cutlass*).   Where?

AGATHA.   It is at our heels.

ERNEST.   Look out, Crichton.

CRICHTON.   H'sh!

> (TREHERNE *comes to his assistance, while*
> LADY MARY *and* CATHERINE *join* AGATHA
> *in the hut.*)

ERNEST.   It will be on us in a moment.

> (*He seizes the hatchet and guards the
> hut.   It is pleasing to see that* ERNEST
> *is no coward.*)

TREHERNE.   Listen!

ERNEST.   The grass is moving.   It's coming.

> (*It comes.   But it is no tiger-cat; it is*
> LORD LOAM *crawling on his hands and*

knees, a very exhausted and dishevelled peer, wondrously attired in rags. The girls see him, and with glad cries rush into his arms.)

LADY MARY. Father.

LORD LOAM. Mary—Catherine—Agatha. Oh dear, my dears, my dears, oh dear!

LADY MARY. Darling.

AGATHA. Sweetest.

CATHERINE. Love.

TREHERNE. Glad to see you, sir.

ERNEST. Uncle, uncle, dear old uncle.

(*For a time such happy cries fill the air, but presently* TREHERNE *is thoughtless.*)

TREHERNE. Ernest thought you were a tiger-cat.

LORD LOAM (*stung somehow to the quick*). Oh, did you? I knew you at once, Ernest; I knew you by the way you ran.

(ERNEST *smiles forgivingly.*)

CRICHTON (*venturing forward at last*). My lord, I am glad.

ERNEST (*with upraised finger*). But you are also idling, Crichton. (*Making himself com-*

fortable on the ground.) We mustn't waste
time. To work, to work.

CRICHTON (*after contemplating him without
rancour*). Yes, sir.

> (*He gets a pot from the hut and hangs it
> on a tripod over the fire, which is now
> burning brightly*.)

TREHERNE. Ernest, you be a little more civil.
Crichton, let me help.

> (*He is soon busy helping* CRICHTON *to
> add to the strength of the hut*.)

LORD LOAM (*gazing at the pot as ladies are
said to gaze on precious stones*). Is that—but
I suppose I'm dreaming again. (*Timidly*.)
It isn't by any chance a pot on top of a fire,
is it?

LADY MARY. Indeed, it is, dearest. It is
our supper.

LORD LOAM. I have been dreaming of a pot
on a fire for two days. (*Quivering*.) There's
nothing in it, is there?

ERNEST. Sniff, uncle. (LORD LOAM *sniffs*.)

LORD LOAM (*reverently*). It smells of onions!

> (*There is a sudden diversion*.)

CATHERINE.   Father, you have boots!

LADY MARY.   So he has.

LORD LOAM.   Of course I have.

ERNEST (*with greedy cunning*).   You are actually wearing boots, uncle.   It's very unsafe, you know, in this climate.

LORD LOAM.   Is it?

ERNEST.   We have all abandoned them, you observe.   The blood, the arteries, you know.

LORD LOAM.   I hadn't a notion.

(*He holds out his feet, and* ERNEST *kneels.*)

ERNEST.   O Lord, yes.

(*In another moment those boots will be his.*)

LADY MARY (*quickly*).   Father, he is trying to get your boots from you.   There is nothing in the world we wouldn't give for boots.

ERNEST (*rising haughtily, a proud spirit misunderstood*).   I only wanted the loan of them.

AGATHA (*running her fingers along them lovingly*).   If you lend them to any one, it will be to us, won't it, father.

LORD LOAM.   Certainly, my child.

ERNEST. Oh, very well. (*He is leaving these selfish ones.*) I don't want your old boots. (*He gives his uncle a last chance.*) You don't think you could spare me *one* boot?

LORD LOAM (*tartly*). I do not.

ERNEST. Quite so. Well, all I can say is I 'm sorry for you.

(*He departs to recline elsewhere.*)

LADY MARY. Father, we thought we should never see you again.

LORD LOAM. I was washed ashore, my dear, clinging to a hencoop. How awful that first night was.

LADY MARY. Poor father.

LORD LOAM. When I woke, I wept. Then I began to feel extremely hungry. There was a large turtle on the beach. I remembered from the *Swiss Family Robinson* that if you turn a turtle over he is helpless. My dears, I crawled towards him, I flung myself upon him —(*here he pauses to rub his leg*)—the nasty, spiteful brute.

LADY MARY. You didn't turn him over?

LORD LOAM (*vindictively, though he is a kindly*

man).   Mary, the senseless thing wouldn't wait;
I found that none of them would wait.

CATHERINE.   We should have been as badly
off if Crichton hadn't——

LADY MARY (*quickly*).   Don't praise Crichton.

LORD LOAM.   And then those beastly monkeys.
I always understood that if you flung stones at
them they would retaliate by flinging cocoa-nuts
at you.   Would you believe it, I flung a hundred
stones, and not one monkey had sufficient
intelligence to grasp my meaning. How I
longed for Crichton.

LADY MARY(*wincing*).   For us also, father?

LORD LOAM.   For you also.   I tried for hours
to make a fire.   The authors say that when
wrecked on an island you can obtain a light by
rubbing two pieces of stick together. (*With
feeling.*)   The liars!

LADY MARY.   And all this time you thought
there was no one on the island but yourself?

LORD LOAM.   I thought so until this morning.
I was searching the pools for little fishes, which I
caught in my hat, when suddenly I saw before
me—on the sand——

CATHERINE. What?

LORD LOAM. A hairpin.

LADY MARY. A hairpin! It must be one of ours. Give it me, father.

AGATHA. No, it's mine.

LORD LOAM. I didn't keep it.

LADY MARY (*speaking for all three*). Didn't keep it? Found a hairpin on an island, and didn't keep it?

LORD LOAM (*humbly*). My dears.

AGATHA (*scarcely to be placated*). Oh father, we have returned to nature more than you bargained for.

LADY MARY. For shame, Agatha. (*She has something on her mind.*) Father, there is something I want you to do at once—I mean to assert your position as the chief person on the island.

(*They are all surprised.*)

LORD LOAM. But who would presume to question it?

CATHERINE. She must mean Ernest.

LADY MARY. Must I?

AGATHA. It's cruel to say anything against Ernest.

LORD LOAM (*firmly*).   If any one presumes to challenge my position, I shall make short work of him.

AGATHA.   Here comes Ernest; now see if you can say these horrid things to his face.

LORD LOAM.   I shall teach him his place at once.

LADY MARY (*anxiously*).   But how?

LORD LOAM (*chuckling*).   I have just thought of an extremely amusing way of doing it.   (*As* ERNEST *approaches.*)   Ernest.

ERNEST (*loftily*).   Excuse me, uncle, I'm thinking.   I'm planning out the building of this hut.

LORD LOAM.   I also have been thinking.

ERNEST.   That don't matter.

LORD LOAM.   Eh?

ERNEST.   Please, please, this is important.

LORD LOAM.   I have been thinking that I ought to give you my boots.

ERNEST.   What!

LADY MARY.   Father.

LORD LOAM (*genially*).   Take them, my boy. (*With a rapidity we had not thought him capable of*, ERNEST *becomes the wearer of the boots*.)   And now I dare say you want to know why I give them to you, Ernest?

ERNEST (*moving up and down in them deliciously*).   Not at all.   The great thing is, 'I 've got 'em, I 've got 'em.'

LORD LOAM (*majestically, but with a knowing look at his daughters*).   My reason is that, as head of our little party, you, Ernest, shall be our hunter, you shall clear the forests of those savage beasts that make them so dangerous.   (*Pleasantly*.)   And now you know, my dear nephew, why I have given you my boots.

ERNEST.   This is my answer.
        (*He kicks off the boots*.)

LADY MARY (*still anxious*).   Father, assert yourself.

LORD LOAM.   I shall now assert myself. (*But how to do it?   He has a happy thought*.) Call Crichton.

LADY MARY.   Oh father.
        (CRICHTON *comes in answer to a summons, and is followed by* TREHERNE.)

ERNEST (*wondering a little at* LADY MARY'S *grave face*). Crichton, look here.

LORD LOAM (*sturdily*). Silence! Crichton, I want your advice as to what I ought to do with Mr. Ernest. He has defied me.

ERNEST. Pooh!

CRICHTON (*after considering*). May I speak openly, my lord?

LADY MARY (*keeping her eyes fixed on him*). That is what we desire.

CRICHTON (*quite humbly*). Then I may say, your lordship, that I have been considering Mr. Ernest's case at odd moments ever since we were wrecked.

ERNEST. My case?

LORD LOAM (*sternly*). Hush.

CRICHTON. Since we landed on the island, my lord, it seems to me that Mr. Ernest's epigrams have been particularly brilliant.

ERNEST (*gratified*). Thank you, Crichton.

CRICHTON. But I find—I seem to find it growing wild, my lord, in the woods, that sayings which would be justly admired in England are not much use on an island. I would therefore most respectfully propose that henceforth every time Mr. Ernest favours us with an epigram his head should be immersed in a bucket of cold spring water.

(*There is a terrible silence.*)

LORD LOAM (*uneasily*).   Serve him right.

ERNEST.   I should like to see you try to do it, uncle.

CRICHTON (*ever ready to come to the succour of his lordship*).   My feeling, my lord, is that at the next offence I should convey him to a retired spot, where I shall carry out the undertaking in as respectful a manner as is consistent with a thorough immersion.

(*Though his manner is most respectful, he is firm; he evidently means what he says.*)

LADY MARY (*a ramrod*).   Father, you must not permit this; Ernest is your nephew.

LORD LOAM (*with his hand to his brow*). After all, he is my nephew, Crichton; and, as I am sure, he now sees that I am a strong man——

ERNEST (*foolishly in the circumstances*).   A

strong man. You mean a stout man. You are one of mind to two of matter.

> (*He looks round in the old way for approval. No one has smiled, and to his consternation he sees that* CRICHTON *is quietly turning up his sleeves.* ERNEST *makes an appealing gesture to his uncle; then he turns defiantly to* CRICHTON.)

CRICHTON. Is it to be before the ladies, Mr. Ernest, or in the privacy of the wood? (*He fixes* ERNEST *with his eye.* ERNEST *is cowed.*) Come.

ERNEST (*affecting bravado*). Oh, all right.

CRICHTON (*succinctly*). Bring the bucket.

> (ERNEST *hesitates. He then lifts the bucket and follows* CRICHTON *to the nearest spring.*)

LORD LOAM (*rather white*). I 'm sorry for him, but I had to be firm.

LADY MARY. Oh father, it wasn't you who was firm. Crichton did it himself.

LORD LOAM. Bless me, so he did.

LADY MARY. Father, be strong.

LORD LOAM (*bewildered*). You can't mean that my faithful Crichton——

LADY MARY. Yes, I do.

TREHERNE. Lady Mary, I stake my word that Crichton is incapable of acting dishonourably.

LADY MARY. I know that; I know it as well as you. Don't you see that that is what makes him so dangerous?

TREHERNE. By Jove, I—I believe I catch your meaning.

CATHERINE. He is coming back.

LORD LOAM (*who has always known himself to be a man of ideas*). Let us all go into the hut, just to show him at once that it is *our* hut.

LADY MARY (*as they go*). Father, I implore you, assert yourself now and for ever.

LORD LOAM. I will.

LADY MARY. And, please, don't ask him how you are to do it—

(CRICHTON *returns with sticks to mend the fire.*)

LORD LOAM (*loftily, from the door of the*

hut). Have you carried out my instructions, Crichton?

CRICHTON (*deferentially*). Yes, my lord.

(ERNEST *appears, mopping his hair, which has become very wet since we last saw him. He is not bearing malice, he is too busy drying, but* AGATHA *is specially his champion.*)

AGATHA. It's infamous, infamous.

LORD LOAM (*strongly*). *My* orders, Agatha.

LADY MARY. Now, father, please.

LORD LOAM (*striking an attitude*). Before I give you any further orders, Crichton——

CRICHTON. Yes, my lord.

LORD LOAM (*delighted*). Pooh! It's all right.

LADY MARY. No. Please go on.

LORD LOAM. Well, well. This question of the leadership; what do you think now, Crichton?

CRICHTON. My lord, I feel it is a matter with which *I* have nothing to do.

LORD LOAM. Excellent. Ha, Mary? That settles it, I think.

LADY MARY. It seems to, but—I 'm not sure.

CRICHTON. It will settle itself naturally, my lord, without any interference from us.

(*The reference to Nature gives general dissatisfaction.*)

LADY MARY. Father.

LORD LOAM (*a little severely*). It settled itself long ago, Crichton, when I was born a peer, and you, for instance, were born a servant.

CRICHTON (*acquiescing*). Yes, my lord, that was how it all came about quite naturally in England. We had nothing to do with it there, and we shall have as little to do with it here.

TREHERNE (*relieved*). That 's all right.

LADY MARY (*determined to clinch the matter*). One moment. In short, Crichton, his lordship will continue to be our natural head.

CRICHTON. I dare say, my lady, I dare say.

CATHERINE. But you must *know*.

CRICHTON. Asking your pardon, my lady, one can't be sure—on an island.

(*They look at each other uneasily.*)

LORD LOAM (*warningly*). Crichton, I don't like this.

CRICHTON (*harassed*).   The more I think of it,
your lordship, the more uneasy I become myself.
When I heard, my lord, that you had left that
hairpin behind——

(*He is pained.*)

LORD LOAM (*feebly*).   One hairpin among so
many would only have caused dissension.

CRICHTON (*very sorry to have to contradict him*).
Not so, my lord.   From that hairpin we could
have made a needle; with that needle we could,
out of skins, have sewn trousers—of which
your lordship is in need; indeed, we are all
in need of them.

LADY MARY (*suddenly self-conscious*).   All?

CRICHTON.   On an island, my lady.

LADY MARY.   Father.

CRICHTON (*really more distressed by the prospect
than she*).   My lady, if Nature does not think
them necessary, you may be sure she will not
ask you to wear them.   (*Shaking his head.*)
But among all this undergrowth——

LADY MARY.   Now you see this man in his
true colours.

LORD LOAM (*violently*).   Crichton, you will

either this moment say, 'Down with Nature,'
or——

CRICHTON (*scandalised*). My Lord!

LORD LOAM (*loftily*). Then this is my last
word to you; take a month's notice.

> (*If the hut had a door he would now
> shut it to indicate that the interview is
> closed.*)

CRICHTON (*in great distress*). Your lordship,
the disgrace——

LORD LOAM (*swelling*). Not another word:
you may go.

LADY MARY (*adamant*). And don't come to
me, Crichton, for a character.

ERNEST (*whose immersion has cleared his
brain*). Aren't you all forgetting that this is an
island?

> (*This brings them to earth with a bump.*
> LORD LOAM *looks to his eldest daughter
> for the fitting response.*)

LADY MARY (*equal to the occasion*). It makes
only this difference—that you may go at once,
Crichton, to some other part of the island.

> (*The faithful servant has been true to*

his superiors ever since he was created,
and never more true than at this moment;
but his fidelity is founded on trust in
Nature, and to be untrue to it would be
to be untrue to them. He lets the wool
he has been gathering slip to the ground,
and bows his sorrowful head. He turns
to obey. Then affection for these great
ones wells up in him.)

CRICHTON. My lady, let me work for you.

LADY MARY. Go.

CRICHTON. You need me so sorely; I can't
desert you; I won't.

LADY MARY (*in alarm, lest the others may
yield*). Then, father, there is but one alterna-
tive, *we* must leave him.

(LORD LOAM *is looking yearningly at*
CRICHTON.)

TREHERNE. It seems a pity.

CATHERINE (*forlornly*). *You* will work for
us?

TREHERNE. Most willingly. But I must
warn you all that, so far, Crichton has done
nine-tenths of the scoring.

LADY MARY. The question is, are we to leave this man?

LORD LOAM (*wrapping himself in his dignity*). Come, my dears.

CRICHTON. My lord!

LORD LOAM. Treherne—Ernest—get our things.

ERNEST. We don't have any, uncle. They all belong to Crichton.

TREHERNE. Everything we have he brought from the wreck—he went back to it before it sank. He risked his life.

CRICHTON. My lord, anything you would care to take is yours.

LADY MARY (*quickly*). Nothing.

ERNEST. Rot! If I could have your socks, Crichton——

LADY MARY. Come, father; we are ready. (*Followed by the others, she and* LORD LOAM *pick their way up the rocks. In their indignation they scarcely notice that daylight is coming to a sudden end.*)

CRICHTON. My lord, I implore you—*I am*

not desirous of being head. Do you have a
try at it, my lord.

LORD LOAM (*outraged*).   A try at it!

CRICHTON (*eagerly*).   It may be that you will
prove to be the best man.

LORD LOAM.   *May* be! My children, come.
(*They disappear proudly in single file.*)

TREHERNE.   Crichton, I'm sorry; but of
course I must go with them.

CRICHTON.   Certainly, sir.
(*He calls to* TWEENY, *and she comes from
behind the hut, where she has been watching
breathlessly.*)

Will you be so kind, sir, as to take her to the
others?

TREHERNE.   Assuredly.

TWEENY.   But what do it all mean?

CRICHTON.   Does, Tweeny, does. (*He passes
her up the rocks to* TREHERNE.) We shall meet
again soon, Tweeny. Good night, sir.

TREHERNE.   Good night. I dare say they
are not far away.

CRICHTON (*thoughtfully*). They went westward,
sir, and the wind is blowing in that direction.

That may mean, sir, that Nature is already taking the matter into her own hands. They are all hungry, sir, and the pot has come a-boil. (*He takes off the lid.*) The smell will be borne westward. That pot is full of Nature, Mr. Treherne. Good night, sir.

TREHERNE.   Good night.

> (*He mounts the rocks with* TWEENY, *and they are heard for a little time after their figures are swallowed up in the fast growing darkness.* CRICHTON *stands motionless, the lid in his hand, though he has forgotten it, and his reason for taking it off the pot. He is deeply stirred, but presently is ashamed of his dejection, for it is as if he doubted his principles. Bravely true to his faith that Nature will decide now as ever before, he proceeds manfully with his preparations for the night. He lights a ship's lantern, one of several treasures he has brought ashore, and is filling his pipe with crumbs of tobacco from various pockets, when the stealthy movements of some animal in the grass startles him.*

With the lantern in one hand and his cutlass in the other, he searches the ground around the hut. He returns, lights his pipe, and sits down by the fire, which casts weird moving shadows. There is a red gleam on his face; in the darkness he is a strong and perhaps rather sinister figure. In the great stillness that has fallen over the land, the wash of the surf seems to have increased in volume. The sound is indescribably mournful. Except where the fire is, desolation has fallen on the island like a pall.

Once or twice, as Nature dictates, CRICHTON *leans forward to stir the pot, and the smell is borne westward. He then resumes his silent vigil.*

Shadows other than those cast by the fire begin to descend the rocks. They are the adventurers returning. One by one they steal nearer to the pot until they are squatted round it, with their hands out to the blaze. LADY MARY *only is absent. Presently she comes within sight of the*

*others, then stands against a tree with her
teeth clenched. One wonders, perhaps,
what Nature is to make of her.)*

End of Act II.

ACT III

ACT III

THE HAPPY HOME

The scene is the hall of their island home two years later. This sturdy log-house is no mere extension of the hut we have seen in process of erection, but has been built a mile or less to the west of it, on higher ground and near a stream. When the master chose this site, the others thought that all he expected from the stream was a sufficiency of drinking water. They know better now every time they go down to the mill or turn on the electric light.

This hall is the living-room of the house, and walls and roof are of stout logs. Across the joists supporting the roof are laid many home-made implements, such as spades, saws, fishing-rods, and from hooks in the joists are suspended cured foods, of which hams are specially in evidence. Deep recesses half way up the walls contain various provender in barrels and sacks. There are some skins, trophies of the chase, on the floor, which is otherwise bare. The chairs and tables are in some cases hewn out of the solid wood,

*and in others the result of rough but efficient carpenter-
ing. Various pieces of wreckage from the yacht have
been turned to novel uses: thus the steering-wheel
now hangs from the centre of the roof, with electric
lights attached to it encased in bladders. A lifebuoy
has become the back of a chair. Two barrels have been
halved and turn coyly from each other as a settee.*

*The farther end of the room is more strictly the
kitchen, and is a great recess, which can be shut off
from the hall by folding doors. There is a large open
fire in it. The chimney is half of one of the boats of
the yacht. On the walls of the kitchen proper are
many plate-racks, containing shells; there are rows
of these of one size and shape, which mark them off
as dinner plates or bowls; others are as obviously
tureens. They are arranged primly as in a well-
conducted kitchen; indeed, neatness and cleanliness
are the note struck everywhere, yet the effect of the
whole is romantic and barbaric.*

*The outer door into this hall is a little peculiar on
an island. It is covered with skins and is in four
leaves, like the swing doors of fashionable restaurants,
which allow you to enter without allowing the hot air
to escape. During the winter season our castaways
have found the contrivance useful, but Crichton's
brain was perhaps a little lordly when he conceived*

*it. Another door leads by a passage to the sleeping-
rooms of the house, which are all on the ground-floor,
and to Crichton's work-room, where he is at this
moment, and whither we should like to follow him,
but in a play we may not, as it is out of sight. There
is a large window space without a window, which,
however, can be shuttered, and through this we have a
view of cattle-sheds, fowl-pens, and a field of grain.
It is a fine summer evening.*

*Tweeny is sitting there, very busy plucking the
feathers off a bird and dropping them on a sheet placed
for that purpose on the floor. She is trilling to herself
in the lightness of her heart. We may remember
that Tweeny, alone among the women, had dressed
wisely for an island when they fled the yacht, and
her going-away gown still adheres to her, though in
fragments. A score of pieces have been added here
and there as necessity compelled, and these have been
patched and repatched in incongruous colours; but,
when all is said and done, it can still be maintained
that Tweeny wears a skirt. She is deservedly proud
of her skirt, and sometimes lends it on important occa-
sions when approached in the proper spirit.*

*Some one outside has been whistling to Tweeny; the
guarded whistle which, on a less savage island, is
sometimes assumed to be an indication to cook that*

*the constable is willing, if the coast be clear. Tweeny,
however, is engrossed, or perhaps she is not in the
mood for a follower, so he climbs in at the window
undaunted, to take her willy nilly. He is a jolly-
looking labouring man, who answers to the name of
Daddy, and— But though that may be his island
name, we recognise him at once. He is Lord Loam,
settled down to the new conditions, and enjoying life
heartily as handy-man about the happy home. He is
comfortably attired in skins. He is still stout, but all
the flabbiness has dropped from him; gone too is his
pomposity; his eye is clear, brown his skin; he
could leap a gate.*

*In his hands he carries an island-made concertina,
and such is the exuberance of his spirits that, as he
lights on the floor, he bursts into music and song, something about his being a chickety chickety chick chick,
and will Tweeny please to tell him whose chickety chick
is she. Retribution follows sharp. We hear a whir,
as if from insufficiently oiled machinery, and over the
passage door appears a placard showing the one word
'Silence.' His lordship stops, and steals to Tweeny
on his tiptoes.*

LORD LOAM. I thought the Gov. was out.

TWEENY. Well, you see he ain't. And if
he were to catch you here idling——

> (LORD LOAM *pales. He lays aside his
> musical instrument and hurriedly dons an
> apron.* TWEENY *gives him the bird to
> pluck, and busies herself laying the table
> for dinner.*)

LORD LOAM (*softly*). What is he doing now?

TWEENY. I think he's working out that
plan for laying on hot and cold.

LORD LOAM (*proud of his master*). And he'll
manage it too. The man who could build a
blacksmith's forge without tools——

TWEENY (*not less proud*). He made the tools.

LORD LOAM. Out of half a dozen rusty
nails. The saw-mill, Tweeny; the speaking-
tube; the electric lighting; and look at the
use he has made of the bits of the yacht that
were washed ashore. And all in two years.
He's a master I'm proud to pluck for.

> (*He chirps happily at his work, and she
> regards him curiously.*)

TWEENY. Daddy, you're of little use, but
you're a bright, cheerful creature to have about

the house. (*He beams at this commendation.*)
Do you ever think of old times now? We
was a bit different.

LORD LOAM (*pausing*). Circumstances alter
cases.

(*He resumes his plucking contentedly.*)

TWEENY. But, Daddy, if the chance was
to come of getting back?

LORD LOAM. I have given up bothering about
it.

TWEENY. You bothered that day long ago
when we saw a ship passing the island. How
we all ran like crazy folk into the water, Daddy,
and screamed and held out our arms. (*They
are both a little agitated.*) But it sailed away,
and we 've never seen another.

LORD LOAM. If we had had the electrical
contrivance we have now we could have
attracted that ship's notice. (*Their eyes rest
on a mysterious apparatus that fills a corner of
the hall.*) A touch on that lever, Tweeny,
and in a few moments bonfires would be blazing
all round the shore.

TWEENY (*backing from the lever as if it might*

spring at her). It's the most wonderful thing he has done.

LORD LOAM (*in a reverie*). And then—England—home!

TWEENY (*also seeing visions*). London of a Saturday night!

LORD LOAM. My lords, in rising once more to address this historic chamber——

TWEENY. There was a little ham and beef shop off the Edgware Road——

> (*The visions fade; they return to the practical.*)

LORD LOAM. Tweeny, do you think I could have an egg to my tea?

> (*At this moment a wiry, athletic figure in skins darkens the window. He is carrying two pails, which are suspended from a pole on his shoulder, and he is* ERNEST. *We should say that he is* ERNEST *completely changed if we were of those who hold that people change. As he enters by the window he has heard* LORD LOAM'S *appeal, and is perhaps justifiably indignant.*)

ERNEST. What is that about an egg? Why should you have an egg?

LORD LOAM (*with hauteur*). That is my affair, sir. (*With a Parthian shot as he withdraws stiffly from the room.*) The Gov. has never put *my* head in a bucket.

ERNEST (*coming to rest on one of his buckets, and speaking with excusable pride. To* TWEENY). Nor mine for nearly three months. It was only last week, Tweeny, that he said to me, 'Ernest, the water cure has worked marvels in you, and I question whether I shall require to dip you any more.' (*Complacently.*) Of course that sort of thing encourages a fellow.

TWEENY (*who has now arranged the dinner table to her satisfaction*). I will say, Erny, I never seen a young chap more improved.

ERNEST (*gratified*). Thank you, Tweeny, that 's very precious to me.

> (*She retires to the fire to work the great bellows with her foot, and* ERNEST *turns to* TREHERNE, *who has come in looking more like a cow-boy than a clergyman.*

He has a small box in his hand which he tries to conceal.)

What have you got there, John?

TREHERNE. Don't tell anybody. It is a little present for the Gov.; a set of razors. One for each day in the week.

ERNEST (*opening the box and examining its contents.*) Shells! He'll like that. He likes sets of things.

TREHERNE (*in a guarded voice*). Have you noticed that?

ERNEST. Rather.

TREHERNE. He's becoming a bit magnificent in his ideas.

ERNEST (*huskily*). John, it sometimes gives me the creeps.

TREHERNE (*making sure that* TWEENY *is out of hearing*). What do you think of that brilliant robe he got the girls to make for him.

ERNEST (*uncomfortably*). I think he looks too regal in it.

TREHERNE. Regal! I sometimes fancy that that's why he's so fond of wearing it. (*Prac-*

tically.) Well, I must take these down to the grindstone and put an edge on them.

ERNEST (*button-holing him*). I say, John, I want a word with you.

TREHERNE. Well?

ERNEST (*become suddenly diffident*). Dash it all, you know, you 're a clergyman.

TREHERNE. One of the best things the Gov. has done is to insist that none of you forget it.

ERNEST (*taking his courage in his hands*). Then—would you, John?

TREHERNE. What?

ERNEST (*wistfully*). Officiate at a marriage ceremony, John?

TREHERNE (*slowly*). Now, that 's really odd.

ERNEST. Odd? Seems to me it 's natural. And whatever is natural, John, is right.

TREHERNE. I mean that same question has been put to me to-day already.

ERNEST (*eagerly*). By one of the women?

TREHERNE. Oh no; they all put it to me long ago. This was by the Gov. himself.

ERNEST. By Jove! (*Admiringly.*) I say, John, what an observant beggar he is.

TREHERNE. Ah! You fancy he was thinking of you?

ERNEST. I do not hesitate to affirm, John, that he has seen the love-light in my eyes. You answered——

TREHERNE. I said Yes, I thought it would be my duty to officiate if called upon.

ERNEST. You 're a brick.

TREHERNE (*still pondering*). But I wonder whether he *was* thinking of you?

ERNEST. Make your mind easy about that.

TREHERNE. Well, my best wishes. Agatha is a very fine girl.

ERNEST. Agatha? What made you think it was Agatha?

TREHERNE. Man alive, you told me all about it soon after we were wrecked.

ERNEST. Pooh! Agatha 's all very well in her way, John, but I 'm flying at bigger game.

TREHERNE. Ernest, which is it?

ERNEST. Tweeny, of course.

TREHERNE. Tweeny? (*Reprovingly.*) Ernest, I hope her cooking has nothing to do with this.

ERNEST (*with dignity*).   Her cooking has very little to do with it.

TREHERNE.   But does she return your affection.

ERNEST (*simply*).   Yes, John, I believe I may say so.   I am unworthy of her, but I think I have touched her heart.

TREHERNE (*with a sigh*).   Some people seem to have all the luck.   As you know, Catherine won't look at me.

ERNEST.   I 'm sorry, John.

TREHERNE.   It 's my deserts; I 'm a second eleven sort of chap.   Well, my heartiest good wishes, Ernest.

ERNEST.   Thank you, John.   How 's the little black pig to-day?

TREHERNE (*departing*).   He has begun to eat again.

> (*After a moment's reflection* ERNEST *calls to* TWEENY.)

ERNEST.   Are you very busy, Tweeny?

TWEENY (*coming to him good-naturedly*). There 's always work to do; but if you want me, Ernest——

ERNEST.   There's something I should like to say to you if you could spare me a moment.

TWEENY.   Willingly.   What is it?

ERNEST.   What an ass I used to be, Tweeny.

TWEENY (*tolerantly*).   Oh, let bygones be bygones.

ERNEST (*sincerely, and at his very best*).   I'm no great shakes even now.   But listen to this, Tweeny; I have known many women, but until I knew you I never knew any woman.

TWEENY (*to whose uneducated ears this sounds dangerously like an epigram*).   Take care—the bucket.

ERNEST (*hurriedly*).   I didn't mean it in that way.   (*He goes chivalrously on his knees.*)   Ah, Tweeny, I don't undervalue the bucket, but what I want to say now is that the sweet refinement of a dear girl has done more for me than any bucket could do.

TWEENY (*with large eyes*).   Are you offering to walk out with me, Erny?

ERNEST (*passionately*).   More than that.   I want to build a little house for you—in the sunny glade down by Porcupine Creek. I want to make chairs for you and tables; and knives and forks, and a sideboard for you.

TWEENY (*who is fond of language*). I like to hear you. (*Eyeing him.*) Would there be any one in the house except myself, Ernest?

ERNEST (*humbly*). Not often; but just occasionally there would be your adoring husband.

TWEENY (*decisively*). It won't do, Ernest.

ERNEST (*pleading*). It isn't as if I should be much there.

TWEENY. I know, I know; but I don't love you, Ernest. I 'm that sorry.

ERNEST (*putting his case cleverly*). Twice a week I should be away altogether—at the dam. On the other days you would never see me from breakfast time to supper.

> (*With the self-abnegation of the true lover.*)

If you like I 'll even go fishing on Sundays.

TWEENY. It 's no use, Erny.

ERNEST (*rising manfully*). Thank you, Tweeny; it can't be helped. (*Then he re-*

members.)   Tweeny, we shall be disappointing the Gov.

TWEENY (*with a sinking*).   What 's that?

ERNEST.   He wanted us to marry.

TWEENY (*blankly*).   You and me? the Gov.! (*Her head droops woefully. From without is heard the whistling of a happier spirit, and* TWEENY *draws herself up fiercely.*)   That 's her; that 's the thing what has stole his heart from me.

> (*A stalwart youth appears at the window, so handsome and tingling with vitality that, glad to depose* CRICHTON, *we cry thankfully, 'The hero at last.' But it is not the hero; it is the heroine. This splendid boy, clad in skins, is what Nature has done for* LADY MARY. *She carries bow and arrows and a blow-pipe, and over her shoulder is a fat buck, which she drops with a cry of triumph. Forgetting to enter demurely, she leaps through the window.*)

(*Sourly.*)   Drat you, Polly, why don't you wipe your feet?

LADY MARY (*good-naturedly*).   Come, Tweeny,
be nice to me.   It 's a splendid buck.

> (*But* TWEENY *shakes her off, and retires
> to the kitchen fire.*)

ERNEST.   Where did you get it?

LADY MARY (*gaily*).   I sighted a herd near
Penguin's Creek, but had to creep round Silver
Lake to get to windward of them.   However, they spotted me and then the fun began.
There was nothing for it but to try and run
them down, so I singled out a fat buck and
away we went down the shore of the lake,
up the valley of rolling stones;   he doubled
into Brawling River and took to the water,
but I swam after him;   the river is only half
a mile broad there, but it runs strong.   He
went spinning down the rapids, down I went
in pursuit;   he clambered ashore, I clambered
ashore;   away we tore helter-skelter up the
hill and down again.   I lost him in the marshes,
got on his track again near Bread Fruit Wood,
and brought him down with an arrow in Firefly
Grove.

TWEENY (*staring at her*).   Aren't you tired?

LADY MARY.   Tired! It was gorgeous.

(*She runs up a ladder and deposits her weapons on the joists. She is whistling again.*)

TWEENY (*snapping*).   I can't abide a woman whistling.

LADY MARY (*indifferently*).   I like it.

TWEENY (*stamping her foot*).   Drop it, Polly, I tell you.

LADY MARY (*stung*).   I won't. I 'm as good as you are.

(*They are facing each other defiantly.*)

ERNEST (*shocked*).   Is this necessary?   Think how it would pain *him*.

(LADY MARY's *eyes take a new expression. We see them soft for the first time.*)

LADY MARY (*contritely*).   Tweeny, I beg your pardon. If my whistling annoys you, I shall try to cure myself of it.

(*Instead of calming* TWEENY, *this floods her face in tears.*)

Why, how can that hurt you, Tweeny dear?

TWEENY.   Because I can't make you lose your temper.

LADY MARY (*divinely*). Indeed, I often do. Would that I were nicer to everybody.

TWEENY. There you are again. (*Wist-fully.*) What makes you want to be so nice, Polly?

LADY MARY (*with fervour*). Only thankful-ness, Tweeny. (*She exults.*) It is such fun to be alive.

> (*So also seem to think* CATHERINE *and* AGATHA, *who bounce in with fishing-rods and creel. They, too, are in manly attire.*)

CATHERINE. We 've got some ripping fish for the Gov.'s dinner. Are we in time? We ran all the way.

TWEENY (*tartly*). You 'll please to cook them yourself, Kitty, and look sharp about it.

> (*She retires to her hearth, where* AGATHA *follows her.*)

AGATHA (*yearning*). Has the Gov. decided who is to wait upon him to-day?

CATHERINE (*who is cleaning her fish*). It 's my turn.

AGATHA (*hotly*). I don't see that.

TWEENY (*with bitterness*). It 's to be neither of you, Aggy; he wants Polly again.

> (LADY MARY *is unable to resist a joyous whistle.*)

AGATHA (*jealously*). Polly, you toad.

> (*But they cannot make* LADY MARY *angry.*)

TWEENY (*storming*). How dare you look so happy?

LADY MARY (*willing to embrace her*). I wish, Tweeny, there was anything I could do to make you happy also.

TWEENY. Me! Oh, I 'm happy. (*She remembers* ERNEST, *whom it is easy to forget on an island.*) I 've just had a proposal, I tell you.

> (LADY MARY *is shaken at last, and her sisters with her.*)

AGATHA. A proposal?

CATHERINE (*going white*). Not—not——

> (*She dare not say his name.*)

ERNEST (*with singular modesty*). You needn't be alarmed; it 's only me.

LADY MARY (*relieved*). Oh, you!

AGATHA (*happy again*). Ernest, you dear, I got such a shock.

CATHERINE. It was only Ernest. (*Showing him her fish in thankfulness.*) They are beautifully fresh; come and help me to cook them.

ERNEST (*with simple dignity*). Do you mind if I don't cook fish to-night? (*She does not mind in the least. They have all forgotten him. A lark is singing in three hearts.*) I think you might all be a little sorry for a chap. (*But they are not even sorry, and he addresses* AGATHA *in these winged words:*) I 'm particularly disappointed in you, Aggy; seeing that I was half engaged to you, I think you might have had the good feeling to be a little more hurt.

AGATHA. Oh, bother.

ERNEST (*summing up the situation in so far as it affects himself*). I shall now go and lie down for a bit.

> (*He retires coldly but unregretted.* LADY MARY *approaches* TWEENY *with her most insinuating smile.*)

LADY MARY. Tweeny, as the Gov. has chosen me to wait on him, please may I have the loan of *it* again?

(*The reference made with such charming delicacy is evidently to* TWEENY'S *skirt.*)

TWEENY (*doggedly*). No, you mayn't.

AGATHA (*supporting* TWEENY). Don't you give it to her.

LADY MARY (*still trying sweet persuasion*). You know quite well that he prefers to be waited on in a skirt.

TWEENY. I don't care. Get one for yourself.

LADY MARY. It is the only one on the island.

TWEENY. And it's mine.

LADY MARY (*an aristocrat after all*). Tweeny, give me that skirt directly.

CATHERINE. Don't.

TWEENY. I won't.

LADY MARY (*clearing for action*). I shall make you.

TWEENY. I should like to see you try.

(*An unseemly fracas appears to be inevitable, but something happens. The whir is again heard, and the notice is displayed 'Dogs delight to bark and bite.' Its effect is instantaneous and cheering. The ladies look at each other guiltily and im-*

mediately proceed on tiptoe to their duties. These are all concerned with the master's dinner. CATHERINE *attends to his fish.* AGATHA *fills a quaint toast-rack and brings the menu, which is written on a shell.* LADY MARY *twists a wreath of green leaves around her head, and places a flower beside the master's plate.* TWEENY *signs that all is ready, and she and the younger sisters retire into the kitchen, drawing the screen that separates it from the rest of the room.* LADY MARY *beats a tom-tom, which is the dinner bell. She then gently works a punkah, which we have not hitherto observed, and stands at attention. No doubt she is in hopes that the Gov. will enter into conversation with her, but she is too good a parlour-maid to let her hopes appear in her face. We may watch her manner with complete approval. There is not one of us who would not give her £26 a year.*

The master comes in quietly, a book in his hand, still the only book on the island, for he has not thought it worth while to build a printing-press. His dress is not noticeably different from that of the others, the skins are similar, but perhaps these are a trifle more carefully cut or he carries them better. One sees somehow that he has changed for his evening meal. There is an odd suggestion of a dinner jacket about his doeskin coat. It is, perhaps, too grave a face for a man of thirty-two, as if he were over much immersed in affairs, yet there is a sunny smile left to lighten it at times and bring back its youth; perhaps too intellectual a face to pass as strictly handsome, not sufficiently suggestive of oats. His tall figure is very straight, slight rather than thick-set, but nobly muscular. His big hands, firm and hard with labour though they be, are finely shaped—note the fingers so much more tapered, the nails better tended than those of his domestics; they are one of many indications that he is of a superior breed. Such signs, as has often been

*pointed out, are infallible. A romantic
figure, too. One can easily see why the
women-folks of this strong man's house
both adore and fear him.*

*He does not seem to notice who is waiting
on him to-night, but inclines his head
slightly to whoever it is, as she takes
her place at the back of his chair. LADY
MARY respectfully places the menu-shell
before him, and he glances at it.)*

CRICHTON. Clear, please.

*(LADY MARY knocks on the screen, and a
serving hutch in it opens, through which
TWEENY offers two soup plates. LADY
MARY selects the clear, and the aperture is
closed. She works the punkah while the
master partakes of the soup.)*

CRICHTON (*who always gives praise where it is
due*). An excellent soup, Polly, but still a
trifle too rich.

LADY MARY. Thank you.

*(The next course is the fish, and while
it is being passed through the hutch we
have a glimpse of three jealous women.*

LADY MARY'S *movements are so deft and noiseless that any observant spectator can see that she was born to wait at table.*)

CRICHTON (*unbending as he eats*). Polly, you are a very smart girl.

LADY MARY (*brindling, but naturally gratified*). La!

CRICHTON (*smiling*). And I 'm not the first you 've heard it from, I 'll swear.

LADY MARY (*wriggling*). Oh Gov.!

CRICHTON. Got any followers on the island, Polly?

LADY MARY (*tossing her head*). Certainly not.

CRICHTON. I thought that perhaps John or Ernest——

LADY MARY (*tilting her nose*). I don't say that it 's for want of asking.

CRICHTON (*emphatically*). I 'm sure it isn't.

(*Perhaps he thinks he has gone too far.*) You may clear.

(*Flushed with pleasure, she puts before him a bird and vegetables, sees that his beaker is filled with wine, and returns to the punkah. She would love to continue their conversation, but it is for him to decide. For a time he seems to have forgotten her.)*

CRICHTON.   Did you lose any arrows to-day?

LADY MARY.   Only one in Firefly Grove.

CRICHTON.   You were as far as that? How did you get across the Black Gorge?

LADY MARY.   I went across on the rope.

CRICHTON.   Hand over hand?

LADY MARY *(swelling at the implied praise)*.   I wasn't in the least dizzy.

CRICHTON *(moved)*.   You brave girl! *(He sits back in his chair a little agitated.)*   But never do that again.

LADY MARY *(pouting)*.   It is such fun, Gov.

CRICHTON *(decisively)*.   I forbid it.

LADY MARY *(the little rebel)*.   I shall.

CRICHTON *(surprised)*.   Polly!

(He signs to her sharply to step forward, but for a moment she holds back petulantly, and even when she does come it is less obediently than like a naughty, sulky child. Nevertheless, with the forbearance that is characteristic of the man, he addresses

> *her with grave gentleness rather than*
> *severely.)*

You must do as I tell you, you know.

LADY MARY (*strangely passionate*).   I shan't.

CRICHTON (*smiling at her fury*).   We shall see.
Frown at me, Polly; there, you do it at once.
Clench your little fists, stamp your feet, bite
your ribbons——

> (*A student of women, or at least of this*
> *woman, he knows that she is about to do*
> *those things, and thus she seems to do*
> *them to order.* LADY MARY *screws up*
> *her face like a baby and cries. He is*
> *immediately kind.*)

You child of Nature; was it cruel of me to
wish to save you from harm?

LADY MARY (*drying her eyes*).   I'm an un-
gracious wretch.   Oh Gov., I don't try half hard
enough to please you.   I'm even wearing—(*she
looks down sadly*)—when I know you prefer *it*.

CRICHTON (*thoughtfully*).   I admit I do prefer
it.   Perhaps I am a little old-fashioned in these
matters.

> (*Her tears again threaten.*)

Ah, don't, Polly; that's nothing.

LADY MARY.   If I could only please you, Gov.

CRICHTON (*slowly*).   You do please me, child, very much—(*he half rises*)—very much indeed. (*If he meant to say more he checks himself. He looks at his plate.*)   No more, thank you.

> (*The simple island meal is ended, save for the walnuts and the wine, and* CRICHTON *is too busy a man to linger long over them. But he is a stickler for etiquette, and the table is cleared charmingly, though with dispatch, before they are placed before him.* LADY MARY *is an artist with the crumb-brush, and there are few arts more delightful to watch. Dusk has come sharply, and she turns on the electric light. It awakens* CRICHTON *from a reverie in which he has been regarding her.*)

CRICHTON.   Polly, there is only one thing about you that I don't quite like.

> (*She looks up, making a moue, if that can be said of one who so well knows her place. He explains.*)

That action of the hands.

LADY MARY.   What do I do?

CRICHTON.   So—like one washing them.   I have noticed that the others tend to do it also. It seems odd.

LADY MARY (*archly*).   Oh Gov., have you forgotten?

CRICHTON.   What?

LADY MARY.   That once upon a time a certain other person did that.

CRICHTON (*groping*).   You mean myself?   (*She nods, and he shudders.*)   Horrible!

LADY MARY (*afraid she has hurt him*).   You haven't for a very long time.   Perhaps it is natural to servants.

CRICHTON.   That must be it.   (*He rises.*) Polly!   (*She looks up expectantly, but he only sighs and turns away.*)

LADY MARY (*gently*).   You sighed, Gov.

CRICHTON.   Did I?   I was thinking.   (*He paces the room and then turns to her agitatedly, yet with control over his agitation.   There is some mournfulness in his voice.*)   I have always tried to do the right thing on this island.   Above all, Polly, I want to do the right thing by you.

LADY MARY (*with shining eyes*).   How we all trust you.   That is your reward, Gov.

CRICHTON (*who is having a fight with himself*). And now I want a greater reward.   Is it fair to you?   Am I playing the game?   Bill Crichton would like always to play the game. If we were in England——

> (*He pauses so long that she breaks in softly.*)

LADY MARY.   We know now that we shall never see England again.

CRICHTON.   I am thinking of two people whom neither of us has seen for a long time— Lady Mary Lasenby, and one Crichton, a butler.

> (*He says the last word bravely, a word he once loved, though it is the most horrible of all words to him now.*)

LADY MARY.   That cold, haughty, insolent girl.   Gov., look around you and forget them both.

CRICHTON.   I had nigh forgotten them.   He has had a chance, Polly—that butler—in these two years of becoming a man, and he has tried

to take it. There have been many failures,
but there has been some success, and with it I
have let the past drop off me, and turned my
back on it. That butler seems a far-away
figure to me now, and not myself. I hail him,
but we scarce know each other. If I am to
bring him back it can only be done by force,
for in my soul he is now abhorrent to me. But
if I thought it best for you I 'd haul him back;
I swear as an honest man, I would bring him
back with all his obsequious ways and deferential
airs, and let you see the man you call your
Gov. melt for ever into him who was your
servant.

LADY MARY (*shivering*). You hurt me. You
say these things, but you say them like a king.
To me it is the past that was not real.

CRICHTON (*too grandly*). A king! I sometimes feel——

> (*For a moment the yellow light gleams in his
> green eyes. We remember suddenly what
> TREHERNE and ERNEST said about his
> regal look. He checks himself.*)

I say it harshly, it is so hard to say, and all

the time there is another voice within me cry-
ing—— (*He stops.*)

LADY MARY (*trembling but not afraid*). If it
is the voice of Nature——

CRICHTON (*strongly*). I know it to be the
voice of Nature.

LADY MARY (*in a whisper*). Then, if you
want to say it very much, Gov., please say it to
Polly Lasenby.

CRICHTON (*again in the grip of an idea*). A
king! Polly, some people hold that the soul
but leaves one human tenement for another, and
so lives on through all the ages. I have occasionally thought of late that, in some past
existence, I may have been a king. It has all
come to me so naturally, not as if I had had to
work it out, but—as—if—I—remembered.

> 'Or ever the knightly years were gone,
>   With the old world to the grave,
> I was a *king* in Babylon,
>   And you were a Christian slave.'

It may have been; you hear me, it may have been.

LADY MARY (*who is as one fascinated*). It may
have been.

CRICHTON. I am lord over all. They are but hewers of wood and drawers of water for me. These shores are mine. Why should I hesitate; I have no longer any doubt. I do believe I am doing the right thing. Dear Polly, I have grown to love you; are you afraid to mate with me? (*She rocks her arms; no words will come from her.*)

> 'I was a king in Babylon,
> And you were a Christian slave.'

LADY MARY (*bewitched*). You are the most wonderful man I have ever known, and I am not afraid.

> (*He takes her to him reverently. Presently he is seated, and she is at his feet looking up adoringly in his face. As the tension relaxes she speaks with a smile.*)

I want you to tell me—every woman likes to know—when was the first time you thought me nicer than the others?

CRICHTON (*who, like all big men, is simple*). I think a year ago. We were chasing goats on the Big Slopes, and you out-distanced us all; you were the first of our party to run a goat down; I was proud of you that day.

LADY MARY (*blushing with pleasure*). Oh Gov., I only did it to please you. Everything I have done has been out of the desire to please you. (*Suddenly anxious.*) If I thought that in taking a wife from among us you were imperilling your dignity——

CRICHTON (*perhaps a little masterful*). Have no fear of that, dear. I have thought it all out. The wife, Polly, always takes the same position as the husband.

LADY MARY. But I am so unworthy. It was sufficient to me that I should be allowed to wait on you at that table.

CRICHTON. You shall wait on me no longer. At whatever table I sit, Polly, you shall soon sit there also. (*Boyishly.*) Come, let us try what it will be like.

LADY MARY. As your servant at your feet.

CRICHTON. No, as my consort by my side.

> (*They are sitting thus when the hatch is again opened and coffee offered. But* LADY MARY *is no longer there to receive*

it.   Her sisters peep through in consterna-
tion. In vain they rattle the cup and saucer.
AGATHA brings the coffee to CRICHTON.)

CRICHTON (forgetting for the moment that it is
not a month hence). Help your mistress first,
girl. (Three women are bereft of speech, but
he does not notice it. He addresses CATHERINE
vaguely.)   Are you a good girl, Kitty?

CATHERINE (when she finds her tongue).   I
try to be, Gov.

CRICHTON (still more vaguely).   That's right.
        (He takes command of himself again,
        and signs to them to sit down. ERNEST
        comes in cheerily, but finding CRICHTON
        here is suddenly weak. He subsides on
        a chair, wondering what has happened.)

CRICHTON (surveying him).   Ernest. (ERNEST
rises.) You are becoming a little slovenly in
your dress, Ernest; I don't like it.

ERNEST (respectfully).   Thank you. (ERNEST
sits again. DADDY and TREHERNE arrive.)

CRICHTON.   Daddy, I want you.

LORD LOAM (with a sinking).   Is it because I
forgot to clean out the dam?

CRICHTON (*encouragingly*).   No, no.   (*He pours some wine into a goblet.*)   A glass of wine with you, Daddy.

LORD LOAM (*hastily*).   Your health, Gov.
> (*He is about to drink, but the master checks him.*)

CRICHTON.   And hers.   Daddy, this lady has done me the honour to promise to be my wife.

LORD LOAM (*astounded*).   Polly!

CRICHTON (*a little perturbed*).   I ought first to have asked your consent.   I deeply regret— but Nature; may I hope I have your approval?

LORD LOAM.   May you, Gov.?   (*Delighted.*) Rather!   Polly!
> (*He puts his proud arms round her.*)

TREHERNE.   We all congratulate you, Gov., most heartily.

ERNEST.   Long life to you both, sir.
> (*There is much shaking of hands, all of which is sincere.*)

TREHERNE.   When will it be, Gov.?

CRICHTON (*after turning to* LADY MARY, *who whispers to him*).   As soon as the bridal skirt can be prepared.   (*His manner has been most indulgent, and without the slightest suggestion of patronage. But he knows it is best for all that he should keep his place, and that his presence hampers them.*) My friends, I thank you for your good wishes, I thank you all. And now, perhaps you would like me to leave you to yourselves. Be joyous. Let there be song and dance to-night. Polly, I shall take my coffee in the parlour—you understand.

> (*He retires with pleasant dignity. Immediately there is a rush of two girls at* LADY MARY.)

LADY MARY. Oh, oh! Father, they are pinching me.

LORD LOAM (*taking her under his protection*). Agatha, Catherine, never presume to pinch your sister again. On the other hand, she may pinch you henceforth as much as ever she chooses.

> (*In the meantime* TWEENY *is weeping softly, and the two are not above using her as a weapon.*)

CATHERINE. Poor Tweeny, it's a shame.

AGATHA. After he had almost promised *you.*

TWEENY (*loyally turning on them*). No, he never did. He was always honourable as could be. 'Twas me as was too vulgar. Don't you dare say a word agin that man.

ERNEST (*to* LORD LOAM). You'll get a lot of tit-bits out of this, Daddy.

LORD LOAM. That's what I was thinking.

ERNEST (*plunged in thought*). I dare say I shall have to clean out the dam now.

LORD LOAM (*heartlessly*). I dare say.

(*His gay old heart makes him again proclaim that he is a chickety chick. He seizes the concertina.*)

TREHERNE (*eagerly*). That's the proper spirit.

(*He puts his arm round* CATHERINE, *and in another moment they are all dancing to Daddy's music. Never were people happier on an island. A moment's pause is presently created by the return of* CRICHTON, *wearing the wonderful robe of which we have already had dark mention. Never has he looked more regal, never perhaps felt so regal. We need not grudge*

*him the one foible of his rule, for it is all
coming to an end.)*

CRICHTON (*graciously, seeing them hesitate*).
No, no; I am delighted to see you all so happy.
Go on.

TREHERNE. We don't like to before you,
Gov.

CRICHTON (*his last order*). It is my wish.

*(The merrymaking is resumed, and soon
CRICHTON himself joins in the dance. It
is when the fun is at its fastest and most
furious that all stop abruptly as if turned
to stone. They have heard the boom of a
gun. Presently they are alive again.
ERNEST leaps to the window.)*

TREHERNE (*huskily*). It was a ship's gun.
*(They turn to CRICHTON for confirmation; even
in that hour they turn to CRICHTON.)* Gov.?

CRICHTON. Yes.

*(In another moment LADY MARY and
LORD LOAM are alone.)*

LADY MARY (*seeing that her father is uncon-
cerned*). Father, you heard.

LORD LOAM (*placidly*). Yes, my child.

LADY MARY (*alarmed by his unnatural calmness*). But it was a gun, father.

LORD LOAM (*looking an old man now, and shuddering a little*). Yes—a gun—I have often heard it. It's only a dream, you know; why don't we go on dancing?

(*She takes his hands, which have gone cold.*)

LADY MARY. Father. Don't you see, they have all rushed down to the beach? Come.

LORD LOAM. Rushed down to the beach; yes, always that—I often dream it.

LADY MARY. Come, father, come.

LORD LOAM. Only a dream, my poor girl.

(CRICHTON *returns. He is pale but firm.*)

CRICHTON. We can see lights within a mile of the shore—a great ship.

LORD LOAM. A ship—always a ship.

LADY MARY. Father, this is no dream.

LORD LOAM (*looking timidly at* CRICHTON). It's a dream, isn't it? There's no ship?

CRICHTON (*soothing him with a touch*). You are awake, Daddy, and there is a ship.

LORD LOAM (*clutching him*). You are not deceiving me?

CRICHTON. It is the truth.

LORD LOAM (*reeling*). True?—a ship—at last!

(*He goes after the others pitifully.*)

CRICHTON (*quietly*). There is a small boat between it and the island; they must have sent it ashore for water.

LADY MARY. Coming in?

CRICHTON. No. That gun must have been a signal to recall it. It is going back. They can't hear our cries.

LADY MARY (*pressing her temples*). Going away. So near—so near. (*Almost to herself.*) I think I 'm glad.

CRICHTON (*cheerily*). Have no fear. I shall bring them back.

(*He goes towards the table on which is the electrical apparatus.*)

LADY MARY (*standing on guard as it were between him and the table*). What are you going to do?

CRICHTON. To fire the beacons.

LADY MARY.   Stop!   (*She faces him.*)   Don't you see what it means?

CRICHTON (*firmly*).   It means that our life on the island has come to a natural end.

LADY MARY (*huskily*).   Gov., let the ship go.

CRICHTON.   The old man—you saw what it means to him.

LADY MARY.   But I am afraid.

CRICHTON (*adoringly*).   Dear Polly.

LADY MARY.   Gov., let the ship go.

CRICHTON (*she clings to him, but though it is his death sentence he loosens her hold*).   Bill Crichton has got to play the game.

> (*He pulls the levers.   Soon through the window one of the beacons is seen flaring red.   There is a long pause.   Shouting is heard.   ERNEST is the first to arrive.*)

ERNEST.   Polly, Gov., the boat has turned back.   They are English sailors;   they have landed!   We are rescued, I tell you, rescued!

LADY MARY (*wanly*).   Is it anything to make so great a to-do about?

ERNEST (*staring*).   Eh?

LADY MARY.   Have we not been happy here?

ERNEST.   Happy? lord, yes.

LADY MARY (*catching hold of his sleeve*). Ernest, we must never forget all that the Gov. has done for us.

ERNEST (*stoutly*).   Forget it?   The man who could forget it would be a selfish wretch and a—— But I say, this makes a difference!

LADY MARY (*quickly*).   No, it doesn't.

ERNEST (*his mind tottering*).   A mighty difference!

> (*The others come running in, some weeping with joy, others boisterous. We see blue-jackets gazing through the window at the curious scene.* LORD LOAM *comes accompanied by a naval officer, whom he is continually shaking by the hand.*)

LORD LOAM.   And here, sir, is our little home. Let me thank you in the name of us all, again and again and again.

OFFICER.   Very proud, my lord.   It is indeed an honour to have been able to assist so distinguished a gentleman as Lord Loam.

LORD LOAM.   A glorious, glorious day.   I

shall show you our other room. Come, my
pets. Come, Crichton.

(*He has not meant to be cruel. He does
not know he has said it. It is the old
life that has come back to him. They
all go. All leave* CRICHTON *except* LADY
MARY.)

LADY MARY (*stretching out her arms to him*).
Dear Gov., I will never give you up.

(*There is a salt smile on his face as he
shakes his head to her. He lets the cloak
slip to the ground. She will not take
this for an answer; again her arms go out
to him. Then comes the great renuncia-
tion. By an effort of will he ceases to be
an erect figure; he has the humble bearing
of a servant. His hands come together
as if he were washing them.*)

CRICHTON (*it is the speech of his life*). My lady.

(*She goes away. There is none to salute
him now, unless we do it.*)

End of Act III.

ACT IV

ACT IV

THE OTHER ISLAND

Some months have elapsed, and we have again the honour of waiting upon Lord Loam in his London home. It is the room of the first act, but with a new scheme of decoration, for on the walls are exhibited many interesting trophies from the island, such as skins, stuffed birds, and weapons of the chase, labelled 'Shot by Lord Loam,' 'Hon. Ernest Woolley's Blow-pipe,' etc. There are also two large glass cases containing other odds and ends, including, curiously enough, the bucket in which Ernest was first dipped, but there is no label calling attention to the incident.

It is not yet time to dress for dinner, and his lordship is on a couch, hastily yet furtively cutting the pages of a new book. With him are his two younger daughters and his nephew, and they also are engaged in literary pursuits; that is to say, the ladies are eagerly but furtively reading the evening papers, of which Ernest is sitting complacently but furtively on an endless number, and doling them out as called for. Note the frequent use of the word 'furtive.' It implies that

*they do not wish to be discovered by their butler, say,
at their otherwise delightful task.*

AGATHA (*reading aloud, with emphasis on the
wrong words*). 'In conclusion, we most heartily
congratulate the Hon. Ernest Woolley. This
book of his, regarding the adventures of himself and his brave companions on a desert isle,
stirs the heart like a trumpet.'

> (*Evidently the book referred to is the one
> in* LORD LOAM'S *hands.*)

ERNEST (*handing her a pink paper*). Here is
another.

CATHERINE (*reading*). 'From the first to the
last of Mr. Woolley's engrossing pages it is
evident that he was an ideal man to be wrecked
with, and a true hero.' (*Large-eyed.*) Ernest!

ERNEST (*calmly*). That's how it strikes *them*,
you know. Here's another one.

AGATHA (*reading*). 'There are many kindly
references to the two servants who were wrecked
with the family, and Mr. Woolley pays the
butler a glowing tribute in a footnote.'

> (*Some one coughs uncomfortably.*)

LORD LOAM (*who has been searching the index for the letter L*). Excellent, excellent. At the same time I must say, Ernest, that the whole book is about yourself.

ERNEST (*genially*). As the author——

LORD LOAM. Certainly, certainly. Still, you know, as a peer of the realm—(*with dignity*)—I think, Ernest, you might have given me one of your adventures.

ERNEST. I say it was you who taught us how to obtain a fire by rubbing two pieces of stick together.

LORD LOAM (*beaming*). Do you, do you? I call that very handsome. What page?

> (*Here the door opens, and the well-bred*
> CRICHTON *enters with the evening papers as subscribed for by the house. Those we have already seen have perhaps been introduced by* ERNEST *up his waistcoat. Every one except the intruder is immediately self-conscious, and when he withdraws there is a general sigh of relief. They pounce on the new papers.* ERNEST *evidently gets a shock from one,*

which he casts contemptuously on the floor.)

AGATHA (*more fortunate*). Father, see page 81. 'It was a tiger-cat,' says Mr. Woolley, 'of the largest size. Death stared Lord Loam in the face, but he never flinched.'

LORD LOAM (*searching his book eagerly*). Page 81.

AGATHA. 'With presence of mind only equalled by his courage, he fixed an arrow in his bow.'

LORD LOAM. Thank you, Ernest; thank you, my boy.

AGATHA. 'Unfortunately he missed.'

LORD LOAM. Eh?

AGATHA. 'But by great good luck I heard his cries'——

LORD LOAM. My cries?

AGATHA. —'and rushing forward with drawn knife, I stabbed the monster to the heart.'

(LORD LOAM *shuts his book with a pettish slam. There might be a scene here were it not that* CRICHTON *reappears and goes to one of the glass cases. All are at once on the alert, and his lordship is particularly sly.)*

LORD LOAM. Anything in the papers, Catherine?

CATHERINE. No, father, nothing—nothing at all.

ERNEST (*it pops out as of yore*). The papers! The papers are guides that tell us what we ought to do, and then we don't do it.

(CRICHTON *having opened the glass case has taken out the bucket, and* ERNEST, *looking round for applause, sees him carrying it off and is undone. For a moment of time he forgets that he is no longer on the island, and with a sigh he is about to follow* CRICHTON *and the bucket to a retired spot. The door closes, and* ERNEST *comes to himself.*)

LORD LOAM (*uncomfortably*). I told him to take it away.

ERNEST. I thought—(*he wipes his brow*)—I shall go and dress.

(*He goes.*)

CATHERINE.   Father, it's awful having Crichton here.   It's like living on tiptoe.

LORD LOAM (*gloomily*).   While he is here we are sitting on a volcano.

AGATHA.   How mean of you! I am sure he has only stayed on with us to—to help us through.   It would have looked so suspicious if he had gone at once.

CATHERINE (*revelling in the worst*).   But suppose Lady Brocklehurst were to get at him and pump him.   She's the most terrifying, suspicious old creature in England; and Crichton simply can't tell a lie.

LORD LOAM.   My dear, that is the volcano to which I was referring. (*He has evidently something to communicate.*) It's all Mary's fault.   She said to me yesterday that she would break her engagement with Brocklehurst unless I told him about—you know what.

(*All conjure up the vision of* CRICHTON.)

AGATHA.   Is she mad?

LORD LOAM.   She calls it common honesty.

CATHERINE.   Father, have you told him?

LORD LOAM (*heavily*). She thinks I have, but I couldn't. She's sure to find out to-night.

> (*Unconsciously he leans on the island concertina, which he has perhaps been lately showing to an interviewer as something he made for* TWEENY. *It squeaks, and they all jump.*)

CATHERINE. It's like a bird of ill-omen.

LORD LOAM (*vindictively*). I must have it taken away; it has done that twice.

> (LADY MARY *comes in. She is in evening dress. Undoubtedly she meant to sail in, but she forgets, and despite her garments it is a manly entrance. She is properly ashamed of herself. She tries again, and has an encouraging success. She indicates to her sisters that she wishes to be alone with papa.*)

AGATHA. All right, but we know what it's about. Come along, Kit.

> (*They go.* LADY MARY *thoughtlessly sits like a boy, and again corrects herself. She addresses her father, but he is in a brown study, and she seeks to draw his*

attention by whistling. This troubles them both.)

LADY MARY. How horrid of me!

LORD LOAM (*depressed*). If you would try to remember——

LADY MARY (*sighing*). I do; but there are so many things to remember.

LORD LOAM (*sympathetically*). There are—(*in a whisper*). Do you know, Mary, I constantly find myself secreting hairpins.

LADY MARY. I find it so difficult to go up steps one at a time.

LORD LOAM. I was dining with half a dozen members of our party last Thursday, Mary, and they were so eloquent that I couldn't help wondering all the time how many of their heads *he* would have put in the bucket.

LADY MARY. I use so many of his phrases. And my appetite is so scandalous. Father, I usually have a chop before we sit down to dinner.

LORD LOAM. As for my clothes—(*wriggling*). My dear, you can't think how irksome collars are to me nowadays.

LADY MARY. They can't be half such an annoyance, father, as——

(*She looks dolefully at her skirt.*)

LORD LOAM (*hurriedly*). Quite so—quite so. You have dressed early to-night, Mary.

LADY MARY. That reminds me; I had a note from Brocklehurst saying that he would come a few minutes before his mother as—as he wanted to have a talk with me. He didn't say what about, but of course we know.

(*His lordship fidgets.*)

(*With feeling.*) It was good of you to tell him, father. Oh, it is horrible to me—(*covering her face*). It seemed so natural at the time.

LORD LOAM (*petulantly*). Never again make use of that word in this house, Mary.

LADY MARY (*with an effort*). Father, Brocklehurst has been so loyal to me for these two years that I should despise myself were I to keep my—my extraordinary lapse from him. Had Brocklehurst been a little less good, then you need not have told him my strange little secret.

LORD LOAM (*weakly*). Polly—I mean Mary —it was all Crichton's fault, he——

LADY MARY (*with decision*). No, father, no; not a word against him though. I haven't the pluck to go on with it; I can't even understand how it ever was. Father, do you not still hear the surf? Do you see the curve of the beach?

LORD LOAM. I have begun to forget—(*in a low voice*). But they were happy days; there was something magical about them.

LADY MARY. It was glamour. Father, I have lived Arabian nights. I have sat out a dance with the evening star. But it was all in a past existence, in the days of Babylon, and I am myself again. But he has been chivalrous always. If the slothful, indolent creature I used to be has improved in any way, I owe it all to him. I am slipping back in many ways, but I am determined not to slip back altogether—in memory of him and his island. That is why I insisted on your telling Brocklehurst. He can break our engagement if he chooses. (*Proudly.*) Mary Lasenby is going to play the game.

LORD LOAM. But my dear——

(LORD BROCKLEHURST *is announced.*)

LADY MARY (*meaningly*). Father, dear, oughtn't you to be dressing?

LORD LOAM (*very unhappy*). The fact is— before I go—I want to say——

LORD BROCKLEHURST. Loam, if you don't mind, I wish very specially to have a word with Mary before dinner.

LORD LOAM. But——

LADY MARY. Yes, father.

> (*She induces him to go, and thus courage-*
> *ously faces* LORD BROCKLEHURST *to hear*
> *her fate.*)

I am ready, George.

LORD BROCKLEHURST (*who is so agitated that she ought to see he is thinking not of her but of himself*). It is a painful matter—I wish I could have spared you this, Mary.

LADY MARY. Please go on.

LORD BROCKLEHURST. In common fairness, of course, this should be remembered, that two years had elapsed. You and I had no reason to believe that we should ever meet again.

> (*This is more considerate than she had expected.*)

LADY MARY (*softening*).   I was so lost to the world, George.

LORD BROCKLEHURST (*with a groan*).   At the same time, the thing is utterly and absolutely inexcusable——

LADY MARY (*recovering her hauteur*).   Oh!

LORD BROCKLEHURST.   And so I have already said to mother.

LADY MARY (*disdaining him*).   You have told her?

LORD BROCKLEHURST.   Certainly, Mary, certainly; I tell mother everything.

LADY MARY (*curling her lip*).   And what did she say?

LORD BROCKLEHURST.   To tell the truth, mother rather pooh-poohed the whole affair.

LADY MARY (*incredulous*).   Lady Brocklehurst pooh-poohed the whole affair!

LORD BROCKLEHURST.   She said, 'Mary and I will have a good laugh over this.'

LADY MARY (*outraged*).   George, your mother is a hateful, depraved old woman.

LORD BROCKLEHURST.   Mary!

LADY MARY (*turning away*).   Laugh in-

deed, when it will always be such a pain
to me.

LORD BROCKLEHURST (*with strange humility*).
If only you would let me bear all the pain,
Mary.

LADY MARY (*who is taken aback*). George,
I think you are the noblest man——

. (*She is touched, and gives him both her
hands. Unfortunately he simpers.*)

LORD BROCKLEHURST. She was a pretty
little thing.

(*She stares, but he marches to his doom.*)
Ah, not beautiful like you. I assure you it
was the merest flirtation; there were a few
letters, but we have got them back. It was
all owing to the boat being so late at Calais.
You see she had such large, helpless eyes.

LADY MARY (*fixing him*). George, when you
lunched with father to-day at the club——

LORD BROCKLEHURST. I didn't. He wired
me that he couldn't come.

LADY MARY (*with a tremor*). But he wrote
you?

LORD BROCKLEHURST. No.

LADY MARY (*a bird singing in her breast*). You haven't seen him since?

LORD BROCKLEHURST. No.

> (*She is saved. Is he to be let off also? Not at all. She bears down on him like a ship of war.*)

LADY MARY. George, who and what is this woman?

LORD BROCKLEHURST (*cowering*). She was— she is—the shame of it—a lady's-maid.

LADY MARY (*properly horrified*). A what?

LORD BROCKLEHURST. A lady's-maid. A mere servant, Mary. (LADY MARY *whirls round so that he shall not see her face.*) I first met her at this house when you were entertaining the servants; so you see it was largely your father's fault.

LADY MARY (*looking him up and down*). A lady's-maid?

LORD BROCKLEHURST (*degraded*). Her name was Fisher.

LADY MARY. My maid!

LORD BROCKLEHURST (*with open hands*). Can you forgive me, Mary?

LADY MARY. Oh George, George!

LORD BROCKLEHURST. Mother urged me not to tell you anything about it; but——

LADY MARY (*from her heart*). I am so glad you told me.

LORD BROCKLEHURST. You see there was nothing wrong in it.

LADY MARY (*thinking perhaps of another incident*). No, indeed.

LORD BROCKLEHURST (*inclined to simper again*). And she behaved awfully well. She quite saw that it was because the boat was late. I suppose the glamour to a girl in service of a man in high position——

LADY MARY. Glamour!—yes, yes, that was it.

LORD BROCKLEHURST. Mother says that a girl in such circumstances is to be excused if she loses her head.

LADY MARY (*impulsively*). George, I am so sorry if I said anything against your mother. I am sure she is the dearest old thing.

LORD BROCKLEHURST (*in calm waters at last*). Of course for women of our class she has a very different standard.

LADY MARY (*grown tiny*).   Of course.

LORD BROCKLEHURST.   You see, knowing how good a woman she is herself, she was naturally anxious that I should marry some one like her. That is what has made her watch your conduct so jealously, Mary.

LADY MARY (*hurriedly thinking things out*).   I know.   I—I think, George, that before your mother comes I should like to say a word to father.

LORD BROCKLEHURST (*nervously*).   About this?

LADY MARY.   Oh no; I shan't tell him of this.   About something else.

LORD BROCKLEHURST.   And you do forgive me, Mary?

LADY MARY (*smiling on him*).   Yes, yes.   I—I am sure the boat was *very* late, George.

LORD BROCKLEHURST (*earnestly*).   It really was.

LADY MARY.   I am even relieved to know that you are not quite perfect, dear.   (*She rests her hands on his shoulders.   She has a moment of contrition.*)   George, when we are married, we shall try to be not an entirely frivolous couple, won't we? We must endeavour to be of some little use, dear.

LORD BROCKLEHURST (*the ass*). *Noblesse oblige.*

LADY MARY (*haunted by the phrases of a better man*). Mary Lasenby is determined to play the game, George.

> (*Perhaps she adds to herself, 'Except just this once.' A kiss closes this episode of the two lovers; and soon after the departure of* LADY MARY *the* COUNTESS OF BROCKLEHURST *is announced. She is a very formidable old lady.*)

LADY BROCKLEHURST. Alone, George?

LORD BROCKLEHURST. Mother, I told her all; she has behaved magnificently.

LADY BROCKLEHURST (*who has not shared his fears*). Silly boy. (*She casts a supercilious eye on the island trophies.*) So these are the wonders they brought back with them. Gone away to dry her eyes, I suppose?

LORD BROCKLEHURST (*proud of his mate*). She didn't cry, mother.

LADY BROCKLEHURST. No? (*She reflects.*) You're quite right. I wouldn't have cried. Cold, icy. Yes, that was it.

LORD BROCKLEHURST (*who has not often contradicted her*). I assure you, mother, that wasn't it at all. She forgave me at once.

LADY BROCKLEHURST (*opening her eyes sharply to the full*). Oh!

LORD BROCKLEHURST. She was awfully nice about the boat being late; she even said she was relieved to find that I wasn't quite perfect.

LADY BROCKLEHURST (*pouncing*). She said that?

LORD BROCKLEHURST. She really did.

LADY BROCKLEHURST. I mean *I* wouldn't. Now if *I* had said that, what would have made me say it? (*Suspiciously.*) George, is Mary all we think her?

LORD BROCKLEHURST (*with unexpected spirit*). If she wasn't, mother, you would know it.

LADY BROCKLEHURST. Hold your tongue, boy. We don't really know what happened on that island.

LORD BROCKLEHURST. You were reading the book all the morning.

LADY BROCKLEHURST. How can I be sure
that the book is true?

LORD BROCKLEHURST. They all talk of it as
true.

LADY BROCKLEHURST. How do I know that
they are not lying?

LORD BROCKLEHURST. Why should they lie?

LADY BROCKLEHURST. Why shouldn't they?
(*She reflects again.*) If I had been wrecked on
an island, I think it highly probable that I
should have lied when I came back. Weren't
some servants with them?

LORD BROCKLEHURST. Crichton, the butler.
    (*He is surprised to see her ring the bell.*)
Why, mother, you are not going to——

LADY BROCKLEHURST. Yes, I am. (*Pointed-
ly.*) George, watch whether Crichton begins any
of his answers to my questions with 'The fact is.'

LORD BROCKLEHURST. Why?

LADY BROCKLEHURST. Because that is usually the beginning of a lie.

LORD BROCKLEHURST (*as* CRICHTON *opens
the door*). Mother, you can't do these things
in other people's houses.

LADY BROCKLEHURST (*coolly, to* CRICHTON). It was I who rang. (*Surveying him through her eyeglass.*) So you were one of the castaways, Crichton?

CRICHTON. Yes, my lady.

LADY BROCKLEHURST. Delightful book Mr. Woolley has written about your adventures. (CRICHTON *bows.*) Don't you think so?

CRICHTON. I have not read it, my lady.

LADY BROCKLEHURST. Odd that they should not have presented you with a copy.

LORD BROCKLEHURST. Presumably Crichton is no reader.

LADY BROCKLEHURST. By the way, Crichton, were there any books on the island?

CRICHTON. I had one, my lady—Henley's poems.

LORD BROCKLEHURST. Never heard of him. (CRICHTON *again bows.*)

LADY BROCKLEHURST (*who has not heard of him either*). I think you were not the only servant wrecked?

CRICHTON. There was a young woman, my lady.

LADY BROCKLEHURST. I want to see her. (CRICHTON *bows, but remains.*) Fetch her up.

(*He goes.*)

LORD BROCKLEHURST (*almost standing up to his mother*). This is scandalous.

LADY BROCKLEHURST (*defining her position*). I am a mother.

> (CATHERINE *and* AGATHA *enter in dazzling confections, and quake in secret to find themselves practically alone with* LADY BROCKLEHURST.)

(*Even as she greets them.*) How d' you do, Catherine—Agatha? You didn't dress like this on the island, I expect! By the way, how did you dress?

> (*They have thought themselves prepared, but*——)

AGATHA. Not—not so well, of course, but quite the same idea.

> (*They are relieved by the arrival of* TREHERNE, *who is in clerical dress.*)

LADY BROCKLEHURST. How do you do, Mr. Treherne? There is not so much of you in the book as I had hoped.

TREHERNE (*modestly*). There wasn't very much of me on the island, Lady Brocklehurst.

LADY BROCKLEHURST. How d' ye mean?

(*He shrugs his honest shoulders.*)

LORD BROCKLEHURST. I hear you have got a living, Treherne. Congratulations.

TREHERNE. Thanks.

LORD BROCKLEHURST. Is it a good one?

TREHERNE. So-so. They are rather weak in bowling, but it 's a good bit of turf.

(*Confidence is restored by the entrance of* ERNEST, *who takes in the situation promptly, and, of course, knows he is a match for any old lady.*)

ERNEST (*with ease*). How do you do, Lady Brocklehurst.

LADY BROCKLEHURST. Our brilliant author!

ERNEST (*impervious to satire*). Oh, I don't know.

LADY BROCKLEHURST. It is as engrossing, Mr. Woolley, as if it were a work of fiction.

ERNEST (*suddenly uncomfortable*). Thanks, awfully. (*Recovering.*) The fact is——

(*He is puzzled by seeing the Brocklehurst family exchange meaning looks.*)

CATHERINE (*to the rescue*). Lady Brocklehurst, Mr. Treherne and I—we are engaged.

AGATHA. And Ernest and I.

LADY BROCKLEHURST (*grimly*). I see, my dears; thought it wise to keep the island in the family.

> (*An awkward moment this for the entrance of* LORD LOAM *and* LADY MARY, *who, after a private talk upstairs, are feeling happy and secure.*)

LORD LOAM (*with two hands for his distinguished guest*). Aha! ha, ha! younger than any of them, Emily.

LADY BROCKLEHURST. Flatterer. (*To* LADY MARY.) You seem in high spirits, Mary.

LADY MARY (*gaily*). I am.

LADY BROCKLEHURST (*with a significant glance at* LORD BROCKLEHURST). After——

LADY MARY. I—I mean. The fact is——

> (*Again that disconcerting glance between the Countess and her son.*)

LORD LOAM (*humorously*). She hears wedding bells, Emily, ha, ha!

LADY BROCKLEHURST (*coldly*). Do you,

Mary? Can't say I do; but I'm hard of hearing.

LADY MARY (*instantly her match*). If you don't, Lady Brocklehurst, I'm sure I don't.

LORD LOAM (*nervously*). Tut, tut. Seen our curios from the island, Emily; I should like you to examine them.

LADY BROCKLEHURST. Thank you, Henry. I am glad you say that, for I have just taken the liberty of asking two of them to step upstairs.

> (*There is an uncomfortable silence, which the entrance of* CRICHTON *with* TWEENY *does not seem to dissipate.* CRICHTON *is impenetrable, but* TWEENY *hangs back in fear.*)

LORD BROCKLEHURST (*stoutly*). Loam, I have no hand in this.

LADY BROCKLEHURST (*undisturbed*). Pooh, what have I done? You always begged me to speak to the servants, Henry, and I merely wanted to discover whether the views you used to hold about equality were adopted on the island; it seemed a splendid opportunity, but Mr. Woolley has not a word on the subject.

> (*All eyes turn to* ERNEST.)

ERNEST (*with confidence*). The fact is——
  (*The fatal words again.*)

LORD LOAM (*not quite certain what he is to assure her of*). I assure you, Emily——

LADY MARY (*as cold as steel*). Father, nothing whatever happened on the island of which I, for one, am ashamed, and I hope Crichton will be allowed to answer Lady Brocklehurst's questions.

LADY BROCKLEHURST. To be sure. There's nothing to make a fuss about, and we're a family party. (*To* CRICHTON.) Now, truthfully, my man.

CRICHTON (*calmly*). I promise that, my lady.
  (*Some hearts sink, the hearts that could never understand a Crichton.*)

LADY BROCKLEHURST (*sharply*). Well, were you all equal on the island?

CRICHTON. No, my lady. I think I may say there was as little equality there as elsewhere.

LADY BROCKLEHURST. All the social distinctions were preserved?

CRICHTON. As at home, my lady.

LADY BROCKLEHURST.   The servants?

CRICHTON.   They had to keep their place.

LADY BROCKLEHURST.   Wonderful.   How was it managed?   (*With an inspiration.*)   You, girl, tell me that?

(*Can there be a more critical moment?*)

TWEENY (*in agony*).   If you please, my lady, it was all the Gov.'s doing.

(*They give themselves up for lost.* LORD LOAM *tries to sink out of sight.*)

CRICHTON.   In the regrettable slang of the servants' hall, my lady, the master is usually referred to as the Gov.

LADY BROCKLEHURST.   I see.   (*She turns to* LORD LOAM.)   You——

LORD LOAM (*reappearing*).   Yes, I understand that is what they call me.

LADY BROCKLEHURST (*to* CRICHTON).   You didn't even take your meals with the family?

CRICHTON.   No, my lady, I dined apart.

(*Is all safe?*)

LADY BROCKLEHURST (*alas*).   You, girl, also? Did you dine with Crichton?

TWEENY (*scared*).   No, your ladyship.

LADY BROCKLEHURST (*fastening on her*). With whom?

TWEENY. I took my bit of supper with—with Daddy and Polly and the rest.

(*Væ victis.*)

ERNEST (*leaping into the breach*). Dear old Daddy—he was our monkey. You remember our monkey, Agatha?

AGATHA. Rather! What a funny old darling he was.

CATHERINE (*thus encouraged*). And don't you think Polly was the sweetest little parrot, Mary?

LADY BROCKLEHURST. Ah! I understand; animals you had domesticated?

LORD LOAM (*heavily*). Quite so—quite so.

LADY BROCKLEHURST. The servants' teas that used to take place here once a month——

CRICHTON. They did not seem natural on the island, my lady, and were discontinued by the Gov.'s orders.

LORD BROCKLEHURST. A clear proof, Loam, that they were a mistake here.

LORD LOAM (*seeing the opportunity for a*

diversion). I admit it frankly. I abandon them. Emily, as the result of our experiences on the island, I think of going over to the Tories.

LADY BROCKLEHURST. I am delighted to hear it.

LORD LOAM (*expanding*). Thank you, Crichton, thank you; that is all.

> (*He motions to them to go, but the time is not yet.*)

LADY BROCKLEHURST. One moment. (*There is a universal but stifled groan.*) Young people, Crichton, will be young people, even on an island; now, I suppose there was a certain amount of—shall we say sentimentalising, going on?

CRICHTON. Yes, my lady, there was.

LORD BROCKLEHURST (*ashamed*). Mother!

LADY BROCKLEHURST (*disregarding him*). Which gentleman? (*To* TWEENY) You, girl, tell me.

TWEENY (*confused*). If you please, my lady——

ERNEST (*hurriedly*). The fact is——

(*He is checked as before, and probably says 'D—n' to himself, but he has saved the situation.*)

TWEENY (*gasping*). It was him—Mr. Ernest, your ladyship.

LADY BROCKLEHURST (*counsel for the prosecution*). With which lady?

AGATHA. I have already told you, Lady Brocklehurst, that Ernest and I——

LADY BROCKLEHURST. Yes, *now;* but you were two years on the island. (*Looking at* LADY MARY). Was it this lady?

TWEENY. No, your ladyship.

LADY BROCKLEHURST. Then I don't care which of the others it was. (TWEENY *gurgles.*) Well, I suppose that will do.

LORD BROCKLEHURST. Do! I hope you are ashamed of yourself, mother. (*To* CRICHTON, *who is going*). You are an excellent fellow, Crichton; and if, after we are married, you ever wish to change your place, come to us.

LADY MARY (*losing her head for the only time*). Oh no, impossible.

LADY BROCKLEHURST (*at once suspicious*). Why impossible? (LADY MARY *cannot answer, or perhaps she is too proud.*) Do you see why it should be impossible, my man?

> (*He can make or mar his unworthy* MARY *now. Have you any doubt of him?*)

CRICHTON. Yes, my lady. I had not told you, my lord, but as soon as your lordship is suited I wish to leave service.

> (*They are all immensely relieved, except poor* TWEENY.)

TREHERNE (*the only curious one*). What will you do, Crichton?

> (CRICHTON *shrugs his shoulders;* 'God knows,' *it may mean.*)

CRICHTON. Shall I withdraw, my lord?

> (*He withdraws without a tremor,* TWEENY *accompanying him. They can all breathe again; the thunderstorm is over.*)

LADY BROCKLEHURST (*thankful to have made herself unpleasant*). Horrid of me, wasn't it? But if one wasn't disagreeable now and again, it would be horribly tedious to be an old woman. He will soon be yours, Mary, and then—think of the opportunities you will have of being disagreeable to me. On that understanding, my dear, don't you think we might——?

(*Their cold lips meet.*)

LORD LOAM (*vaguely*). Quite so—quite so.

(CRICHTON *announces dinner, and they file out.* LADY MARY *stays behind a moment and impulsively holds out her hand.*)

LADY MARY. To wish you every dear happiness.

CRICHTON (*an enigma to the last.*) The same to you, my lady.

LADY MARY. Do you despise me, Crichton? (*The man who could never tell a lie makes no answer.*) You are the best man among us.

CRICHTON. On an island, my lady, perhaps; but in England, no.

LADY MARY. Then there's something wrong with England.

CRICHTON. My lady, not even from you can I listen to a word against England.

LADY MARY.   Tell me one thing: you have not lost your courage?

CRICHTON.   No, my lady.

(*She goes.   He turns out the lights.*)